THE ROUGH GUIDE TO THE
A-Z OF TRAVEL

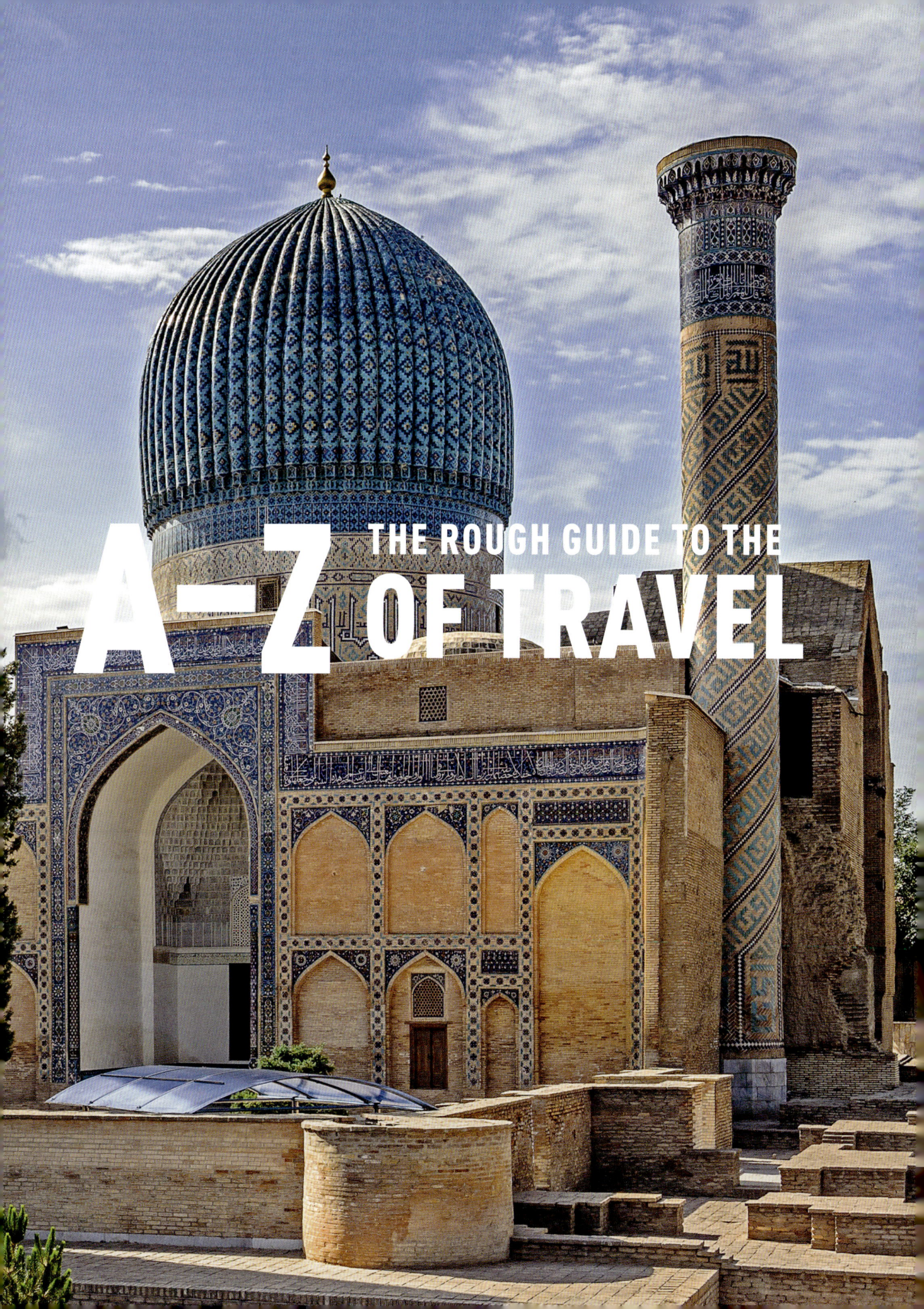

THE ROUGH GUIDE TO THE
A–Z OF TRAVEL

DISTRIBUTION

UK, Ireland and Europe
Apa Publications (UK) Ltd; sales@roughguides.com

United States and Canada
Ingram Publisher Services; ips@ingramcontent.com

Australia and New Zealand
Booktopia; retailer@booktopia.com.au

Worldwide
Apa Publications (UK) Ltd; sales@roughguides.com

SPECIAL SALES, CONTENT LICENSING AND CO-PUBLISHING

Rough Guides can be purchased in bulk quantities at discounted prices. We can create special editions, personalized jackets and corporate imprints tailored to your needs. Email: sales@roughguides.com
roughguides.com

Printed in Czech Republic

A catalogue record for this book is available from the British Library

The publishers and authors have done their best to ensure the accuracy and currency of all the information in *The Rough Guide to the A–Z of Travel*, however, they can accept no responsibility for any loss, injury, or inconvenience sustained by any traveller as a result of information or advice contained in the guide.

HELP US UPDATE

We've gone to a lot of effort to ensure that this first edition of *The Rough Guide to the A–Z of Travel* is accurate and up to date. But if you feel we've got it wrong or left something out, we'd like to know.
Please send your comments with the subject line "Rough Guide to the A–Z of Travel" to mail@uk.roughguides.com. We'll credit all contributions and send a copy of the next edition (or any other Rough Guide if you prefer) for the very best emails.

THE ROUGH GUIDE TO THE
A-Z OF TRAVEL

Commissioning Editor: Joanna Reeves
Proofreader: Annie Warren
Original concept: Zara Sekhavati
Picture Editor: Piotr Kala
Designer: Pradeep Thapliyal
Head of DTP and Pre-press: Rebeka Davies
Head of Publishing: Sarah Clark

A–Z

THE ROUGH GUIDE TO THE
OF TRAVEL

INTRODUCTION

Travel is a luxury. If money is no object, the world is indeed your oyster. But if you're backpacking on a shoestring, how can you rack up passport stamps without breaking the bank? Enter, our A–Z of destinations for every budget. From a wallet-friendly city break in Ghent to a no-expense-spared adventure in Bhutan's Bumthang Valley, our Rough Guides experts have scoped out some of the most beautiful, fascinating and curious corners of the globe. Far-flung escapes beckon on Easter Island and Faial, history pervades Matera's ancient *sassi*, and extraordinary architecture abounds in the rock-hewn churches of Lalibela. Destinations are categorised by the following daily budget (excluding travel):

Shoestring: under £80
Save: £80-160
Splurge: over £160

This list is by no means exhaustive, but we hope to provide inspiration for your travels. Please tag us with any of your own destination ideas using the hashtag #RoughGuideAtoZ; we'd love to hear from you.

Joanna Reeves, Editor

The glorious guildhouses of Grote Markt

ANTWERP, BELGIUM

SHOESTRING Antwerp – Belgium's second city – has long lured the cool crowd to its cultural scene. The Antwerp Six led the style revolution in the 1980s, and their legacy lives on in a thriving fashion district, home to the world-class ModeMuseum (MoMu). Modern art takes centre stage in the Museum of Contemporary Art (M HKA) and independent galleries like Zeno X, Annie Gentils and De Zwarte Panter. Despite its ahead-of-the-curve credentials, Antwerp has a rich historic legacy, from its medieval core and riverside fortress to its magnificent cathedral hung with masterpieces by the city's most famous son: long-term resident Rubens.

Stay: *YUST Antwerp* is a design-forward hostel on the outskirts of the city, close to De Koninck brewery, with edgy interiors and a concept restaurant.

Eat: For cheap fast food, try the kebab and falafel places on Oude Koornmarkt, or any of the *frituurs*. Head to *Fritkot Max* for the best chips in town or *Kapitein Zeppos* for its excellent-value *dagschotel* (daily special).

Drink: After hours, hotfoot it to *Ampere* beneath the railway tracks, which aims to mimic Berlin's underground music scene.

Rubenshuis, the former home and studio of Rubens

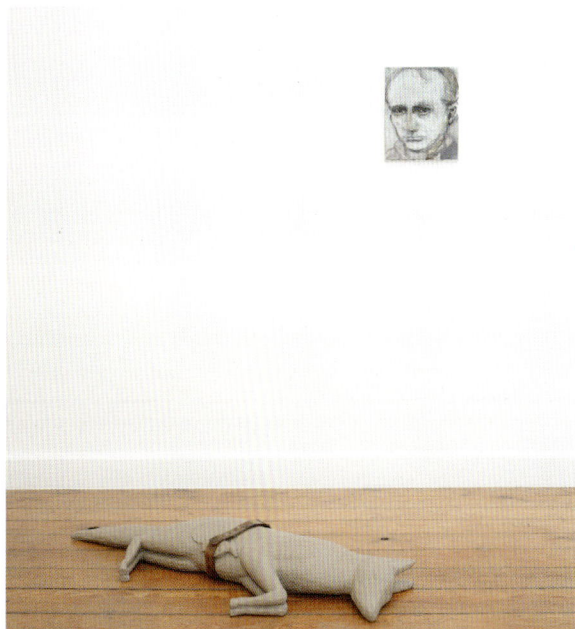

Zeno X Gallery specialises in figurative art

Het Steen, Antwerp's medieval fortress

E/MOTION: Fashion in Transition exhibition in MoMu

The Granite City has a surprisingly sandy beach

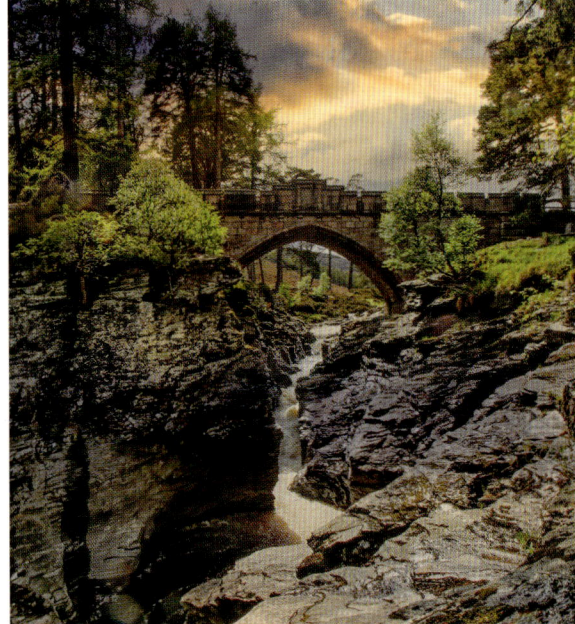

The Linn of Dee, near Braemar

Aberdeen Art Gallery, home to one of the UK's finest collections

Footdee is a historic fishing village in Aberdeen

ABERDEEN, SCOTLAND

SAVE Staring down the North Sea with a defiant gaze, Aberdeen is one of the UK's northernmost cultural hubs and a staging post for explorations of the superlative landscape of Aberdeenshire. The city's distinctive granite buildings – moody grey in winter, glistening silver in the sun – seem cut from a single slab of rock, broken only by the vibrant end-of-terrace murals put up during the annual Nuart street art festival. The beach is long and – unexpectedly for such a stony city – sandy. Follow it down to the artisanal shops and artist-run galleries in the quaint fishing village of Footdee (pronounced 'Fittie') and the dolphin-spotting perch at Torry Battery. When the mountains call, take the #201 bus along the River Dee into the Cairngorms, hopping off for the charming hiking gateway towns of Ballater and Braemar.

Stay: Check into *Lochnagar Guest House* for characterful central lodgings.

Eat: Kickstart the day with breakfast butteries – traditional savoury rolls, something like a squashed croissant – from *Ross Bakery* on Chapel Street.

Drink: The oldest pub in town, *Ma Cameron's* is a firm favourite with locals for a wee dram; nab a seat on the rooftop terrace in the summer.

The Iceberg building, Aarhus Ø

AARHUS, DENMARK

SPLURGE The Jutland peninsula, known for its historic towns, natural landscapes and wide-open skies, can seem sleepy in contrast to Copenhagen. But it's also home to Denmark's second-largest city, Aarhus, with its cutting-edge museums, innovative architecture and culinary clout. The small but cosmopolitan city has an atmospheric historic core, with many buildings dating to the Middle Ages. To see the city's modern face, cycle around the Aarhus Ø development, where iceberg-like buildings slice out into the cold waters of the bay. Be sure to immerse yourself in Aarhus' creative life, viewing contemporary art at the ARoS museum or picking up local pieces at the galleries and craft workshops of Godsbanen and the Latin Quarter.

Stay: The eco-friendly *Scandic* has a great location near ARoS, while *SOFS* is a boutique hotel is in the heart of the city's shopping and nightlife action.

Eat: Head to *Hærværk* for upscale, inventive Danish cuisine and a focus on sustainability that has earned the team a Michelin Green Star.

Drink: Keep an eye out in bars and shops for Njord craft gin, produced in a restored red-brick brewery in the Sydhavnen district.

The city is threaded by the Aarhus River

Your rainbow panorama, designed by artist Olafur Eliasson, ARoS

Njord produces a popular local gin

ARoS is filled with ten floors of contemporary art

B

Quaint stone buildings in Bansko old town

МЕХАНА
КАДИЯТА

BANSKO, BULGARIA

SHOESTRING For a budget-friendly ski destination in Europe, you can't beat Bansko. Just two hours from Sofia, this lesser-visited Bulgarian resort offers skiing and snowboarding at a fraction of the price of its big-hitting cousins in France, Austria and Switzerland. Seventy-five kilometres of marked pistes reach altitudes of up to 2500m, wending between the Unesco-protected Pirin Mountains. The slopes are best suited to intermediates; mainly blues and reds, plus one steep black. The quaint old town is a knot of tangled streets lined with stone-built buildings, many reimagined as bars, restaurants and shops. Beyond the pistes, wallow in the Regnum Banya hot springs, visit the Unesco-listed Rila Monastery or venture to Plovdiv, a 2019 European Capital of Culture.

Stay: Head to *Le Retro Hostel, Bar & Bistro*, a cosy spot in the village square, or *Casa Karina* for a slightly more luxe feel without breaking the bank.

Eat: The old town is peppered with traditional *mehanas* (pubs) serving up hearty local specialties; try *Mehana Chevermeto*.

Drink: With beer up for grabs at £1.50 a pint in most pubs, you'll certainly be thankful of the fresh mountain air the morning after the night before.

Bansko: a wallet-friendly alternative for skiers

Banski chomlek, a traditional Bulgarian stew

Rila Monastery, a Unesco World Heritage Site

Ski runs reach altitudes of up to 2500m

Széchenyi Baths

Lángos, a Hungarian speciality

Gerlóczy, a budget hotel and brasserie

Great Market Hall, built in 1897

BUDAPEST, HUNGARY

SAVE Bisected by the Danube River, Budapest is a city of two halves, connected since 1849 by the iconic Széchenyi Chain Bridge. On the western banks, the hills of Buda cradle the cobblestone medieval quarter and its grand palace and colourful tile-roofed Matthias Church. To the east is buzzy Pest, with its domed Parliament building and cluster of cafés, shops and bars. Discover the city's heritage in the Budapest History Museum, feast on *lángos* (deep-fried bread topped with cheese, sour cream and garlic sauce) in the Great Market Hall, and party into the small hours at a cool ruin bar. Blow away cobwebs at Széchenyi Baths, a huge complex of indoor and outdoor thermal pools filled with mineral-rich therapeutic waters.

Stay: Above a café of the same name, *Gerlóczy* is one of the city's best-value hotels, especially if you can nab one of the slightly cheaper attic rooms.

Eat: Book a table at *Café Kör*, a local favourite serving up Hungarian classics.

Drink: *Szimpla Kert* is one of the original ruin bars, with live DJs, a labyrinth of junk-filled bars, and a buzzy vibe.

Celebrations for the Jampa Lhakhang Drup festival

BUMTHANG VALLEY, BHUTAN

SPLURGE The idyllic Bumthang Valley in the Bhutan Himalaya is studded with Buddhist temples and monasteries. The most significant of these is the Kurjey Lhakhang, a vast monastery complex that shelters the cave where Indian Buddhist Guru Rinpoche once meditated, and a narrow rock passage said to rid anyone who can crawl through it of all their earthly sins. Immerse yourself in local customs by sinking into a Bhutanese hot stone bath, filled with river water heated using rocks roasted on a fire and scattered with herbal artemisia leaves. Visit in October for the Jampa Lhakhang Drup, a four-day festival involving a mewing (fire blessing) during which pilgrims leap through a burning archway.

Stay: Exuding subtle sophistication, *Amankora* is filled with a cluster of elegant rooms, all with underfloor heating, shag-pile rugs and open-plan bathrooms centred around a freestanding bath.

Eat: Visitors to Bhutan typically eat in their accommodation, though a smatte-ring of places fulfils travellers on the move.

Drink: There are no bars in this corner of Bhutan, but most of the Western hotels serve tipples to guests.

Kurje Lhakhang, one of the most sacred sites in Bhutan

Monks rehearsing for the Jakar Tshechu Festival

Amankora, a luxurious bolthole in Thimphu

C

Bookseller at the Güemes flea market

Güemes is popular with university students

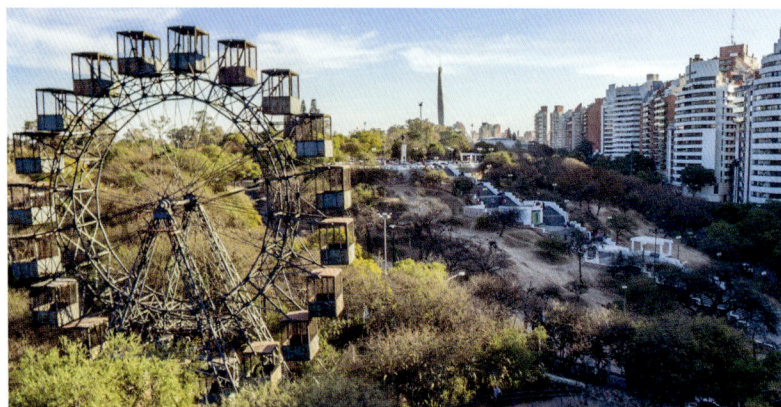
Sarmiento Park, a lush green space in the city

Traslasierra Valley drums to a slower beat

CÓRDOBA, ARGENTINA

SHOESTRING Argentina's second city and capital of the eponymous province, Córdoba is bursting with vibrant sixteenth-century history, brought up to date by fun-loving *córdobeses*. Unfurling from the banks of the Suquía River, it's an easy city to walk around, taking in sights such as the Manzana Jesuítica (Jesuit Block), Los Capuchinos church and Sarmiento Park. Students choose Córdoba – the first city in Argentina to found a state university – for its buzzy nightlife; go-to neighbourhood Barrio Güemes is home to a warren of passageways sheltering cocktail bars and clubs. In February, iconic folk festival Cosquín Rock attracts big-name musicians like Soledad. Beyond the city, Traslasierra Valley's vine-combed hills attract Buenos Aires hipsters and oenophiles after an easy pace and locally grown Malbec, while Villa Tulumba to the north is an outdoor playground for mountain bikers and trekkers.

Stay: Rest your head at *Casa Bucanaan*, a friendly hostel just a short walk from the Jesuit Block.

Eat: Enjoy authentic Armenian dishes at *Dirán*, tucked away inside the Mercado Municipal, for lunch.

Drink: For a refreshing pint of locally brewed craft beer, stop by the roof terrace at *Höppers*.

The Unesco-listed Manzana Jesuítica church

Carnlough Harbour

Pastoral scenes in Glenshesk

Fair Head offers fine views towards Rathlin Island and beyond

Glenariff Nature Reserve Waterfalls Walk

CAUSEWAY COAST, NORTHERN IRELAND

SAVE A drive through the Glens of Antrim is full of drama: dense forests give way to hidden waterfalls and glacier-gouged valleys – *Game of Thrones* fans are sure to recognise some of the locations. Flanked by towering cliffs, the Atlantic-sculpted Causeway Coast is studded with some of Northern Ireland's prettiest villages. Carnlough is a charming jumble of limestone houses, while further north, the colour-washed buildings of Cushendall are strung prettily along the waterfront. Fair Head is a must for sublime views across the North Channel to Scotland's Mull of Kintyre, Islay and the Paps of Jura. Rathlin Island is a tempting diversion for birdwatching hikes, or bypass a boat trip in favour of the legend-steeped Giant's Causeway. Finish in Portstewart with its ruined castle – inspiration for Cair Paravel in C.S. Lewis' *Chronicles of Narnia*.

Stay: Right on the water's edge, *Cushendall Caravan Park* is a scenic campsite with powered sites, tent pitches and wooden pods.

Eat: Popular *Harry's* in Cushendall dishes up good-value, big-portion meals.

Drink: Don't miss *Johnny Joe's*, a convivial pub in Cushendall with live music.

Mighty Machu Picchu

CUSCO, PERU

SPLURGE Arriving in Cusco, at 3339m above sea level, is – quite literally – breathtaking. The historic capital of the powerful yet short-lived Inca Empire, this captivating city is scattered with the architectural remains of ceremonial centres such as Sacsayhuamán and Qorikancha. The Spanish conquistadors may have destroyed many religious temples, but the Inca's fitted masonry still forms the foundations of many buildings lining the narrow alleys of the old town. Before taking the train to visit the iconic Machu Picchu, acclimatise in the quaint village of Ollantaytambo in the Sacred Valley, at a considerably lower 2300 metres. This fertile valley, fed by the Urubamba River, was the natural pantry that powered the Inca army. Today, farmers still cultivate the land, which is dotted with archaeological sites such as Moray and Pisac.

Stay: For a slice of luxury, check into *Monasterio, A Belmond Hotel* in Cusco.

Eat: Book a table at *Mil*, the Andean restaurant from award-winning Peruvian husband-and-wife chef team Virgilio Martínez and Pía León.

Drink: Savour a pint of craft beer at the *Cerveceria del Valle Sagrado*, a cool taproom near Ollantaytambo.

ocals in Ollantaytambo, a village in the Sacred Valley

Monasterio, A Belmond Hotel

laza de Armas, Cusco

Farm-to-fork dining at *Mil*

D

Lush tea plantations in Darjeeling

DARJEELING, INDIA

SHOESTRING Clinging to a 2200m-high ridge in the northern reaches of West Bengal, Darjeeling offers a budget-friendly taste of the mighty Himalayas. The foreboding silhouette of immortal giant Kanchenjunga – the third-highest peak in the world at 8586m – looms all over town, best seen from Tiger Hill at sunrise. Darjeeling is famed not just for its rolling tea estates – the legacy of nineteenth-century British colonisation – but also for the Himalayan Railway fondly known as Toy Train. Built in 1881, this Unesco-listed 2ft gauge railway still operates one of the world's last working steam trains. If you don't fancy the tourist ride to Ghum, wait for the locomotive to pop and chug on the main road to town, skirting shops and people by inches as it makes its way into Darjeeling's diminutive train station.

Stay: *Hideout Backpackers Hostel* offers clean dorms with shared bathrooms, plus there's a social vibe and a nice rooftop with superb mountain views.

Eat: Family-run *Chekey's House* is a locals' favourite for Tibetan food.

Drink: Locals and travellers flock to *Gatty's Café* for live music, while *Joey's* is a small, intimate pub renowned for its beer, ambience and chat.

Peace Pagoda in Darjeeling

Street-food stalls line the streets

Picking *camellia sinensis* (tea plant) by hand

The Darjeeling Himalayan Railway, or Toy Train

Rocky Mountain Arsenal National Wildlife Refuge, near Denver

Union Station, home to restaurants and a farmers' market

Street-food stands line the mile-long 16th Street Mall

Street performer at the 16th Street Mall

The 40ft-high *I see what you mean* sculpture in Downtown

DENVER, USA

SAVE With its impossible-to-miss ensemble of gleaming skyscrapers, Denver marks the final transition from the Great Plains and the American West, sitting at the threshold of the Rocky Mountains. At an elevation of 5280ft, the aptly named mile-high city was founded on a gold rush in 1858. Downtown is a seriously cool enclave, bisected by the pedestrianised mile-long 16th Street Mall, peppered with food carts, bars and painted pianos. Here, you'll also find one of the States' best independent bookstores: the Tattered Cover, set in a restored 1896 warehouse opposite Union Street station.

Stay: Hunker down in *The Queen Anne*, an eco-friendly B&B with individually decorated rooms.

Eat: *Casa Bonita* has been plating up Mexican food since 1974; don't miss the all-you-can-eat deluxe dinners.

Drink: In business since 1873, *My Brother's Bar* is where Jack Kerouac would visit Neal Cassady in the 1950s.

DUBLIN, IRELAND

SPLURGE Confident capital Dublin has a raw, modern energy complemented by rich cultural traditions. Medieval monuments rub shoulders with world-class galleries and museums. Don't miss the richly varied exhibits of the National Gallery and National Museum before heading to Trinity College to admire the ninth-century *Book of Kells* and magnificent Long Room. For those with deep pockets, Grafton Street is a shopper's paradise while an epicurean enclave has emerged around the George's Street and South William Street area.

Stay: *The Westbury* is a five-star beauty brimming with understated luxury.

Eat: The table to book is at *Restaurant Patrick Guilbaud*, which has scooped two Michelin stars for its contemporary Irish cuisine with a French classical twist.

Drink: Sip a pint of Guinness in the *Palace Bar*, a traditional drinking den and the former haunt of writers Behan, Kavanagh and Flann O'Brien.

The Old Library, home to the *Book of Wells*

Dublin's streets are lively with pavement cafés and restaurants

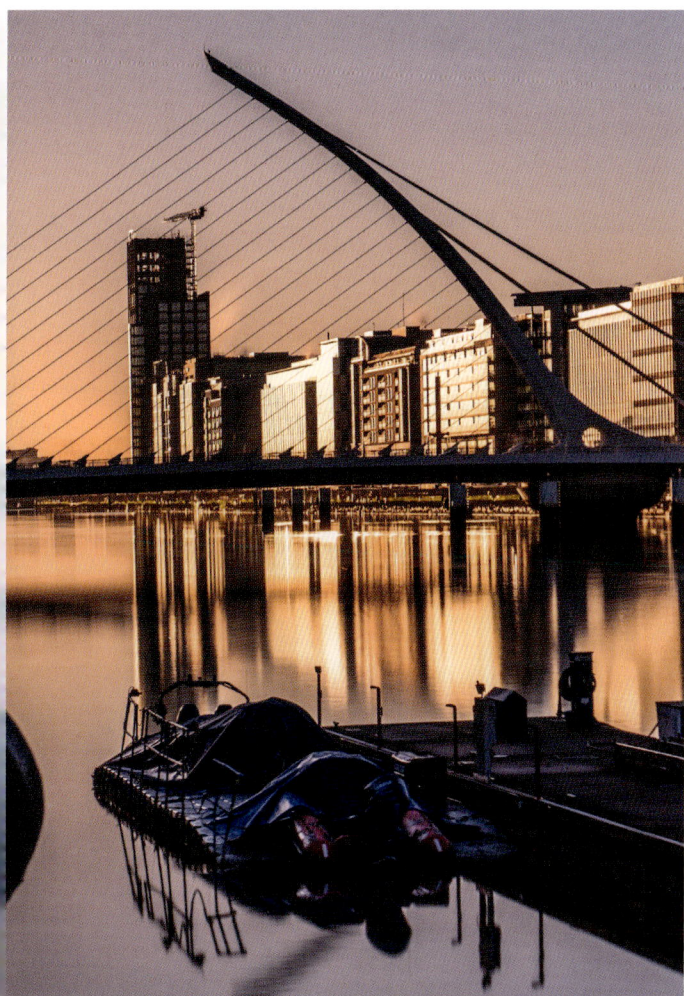

Samuel Beckett Bridge straddles the River Liffey

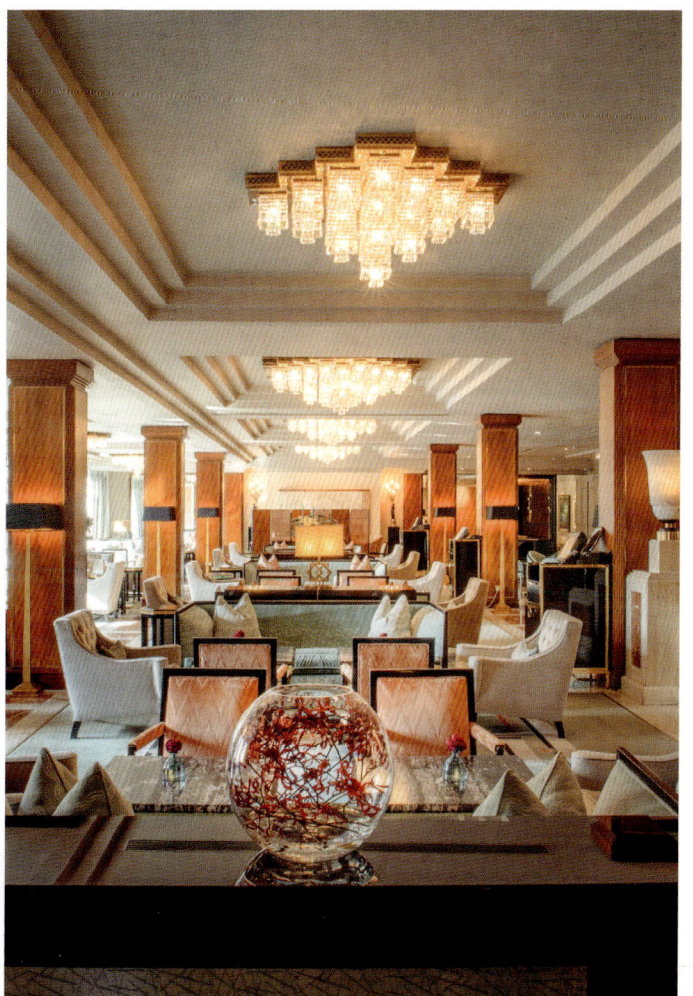

The Westbury: a slice of luxury

E

Old stone walls wrap around the ancient medina

Menus are dominated by locally caught seafood

Tiny restaurants spill out into colour-washed lanes

The Atlantic swell lures kitesurfers to Essaouira

ESSAOUIRA, MOROCCO

SHOESTRING Dating back to the eighteenth century, Essaouira became popular with hippies and musicians in the 1960s (Jimi Hendrix and Cat Stevens visited) before growing up into the upmarket destination it is today. Against the backdrop of fishermen repairing nets on the harbourfront, whitewashed restaurants serve catch of the day to diners on the water's edge. Kite- and windsurfers flock to the Windy City, so called for the *alizee* that whips this stretch of Atlantic coastline. Duck inside the fortified walls to wander the ancient medina or browse the contemporary art galleries. Visit in June to catch the Gnaoua World Music Festival, featuring global stars and *gnaoua* masters who keep alive the ancient African Islamic music tradition.

Stay: Try *Riad du Figuier*, set around a courtyard planted with orange trees.

Eat: You can't do much better than eat at the line of grills down at the port, where that day's fresh seafood might include squid or snapper.

Drink: *Taros* is the best evening venue in town, with live music on a rooftop terrace overlooking the main square.

Views over the historic core of Eger

EGER, HUNGARY

SAVE Wedged between the Mátra and Bükk mountain ranges in the forested Northern Uplands, Eger lays fair claim to the title of Hungary's most attractive town. Its history is as turbulent as it is long, pieced together by a jigsaw of architectural styles. The old medieval square, Dobó tér, and the surrounding streets are littered with buildings from different eras: a Neoclassical cathedral painted in the favourite Hungarian yellow; the Baroque Archbishop's Palace; a muscular fortress that heroically repelled Ottoman attack in 1552 – although the Turks did return a few years later and laid waste to the town; and the most northerly minaret in the former Ottoman Empire.

Stay: Retire to the warming sanctity of *Hotel Senator-Ház*, which occupies a 300-year-old building on the main square.

Eat: You can dine well, and affordably, at *Macok*, a convivial bistro serving the likes of trout from nearby Szilvásvárad and wild boar from the local hills.

Drink: Don't miss the wine cellars in the "Valley of the Beautiful Women" (Szépasszony-völgy), where private vintners will cheerfully pour you generous measures of the region's famous red wine, Egri Bikavér, or Bull's Blood.

Statue of István Dobó, defender of Eger against the Ottomans in 1552

Local cellers are best known for Egri Bikavér wine

Narrow lanes are lined by pastel-hued buildings

Eger is home to the Ottoman Empire's northernmost minaret

Polynesian dance performance at Anakena beach

Boat-fresh *ceviche* is a local favourite

View from the summit of Rano Kau volcano

Rano Raraku quarry supplied the stone used for Moai

EASTER ISLAND, CHILE

SPLURGE Cast adrift 3700km from mainland Chile, Easter Island is the world's most remote inhabited archipelago. Its Polynesian culture is striking: stoic Moai statues solemnly stand on *ahu* platforms, their origins largely inexplicable. Even today, it is not known why the islanders carved such colossal sculptures or how they moved and raised them onto rocky slabs. Half the island falls under national park status, a rugged landscape littered with archaeological sites and sculpted by volcanic cones. Trekking and outdoor adventures await in Anakena and Rano Kau, while the pristine ocean lapping the island's shores is ideal for underwater adventures. The climate is mild year-round but February is a particularly great time to visit, when islanders celebrate Tapati, a two-week festival that embraces traditional Rapa Nui culture.

Stay: The fabulous eco-lodge *Explora Rapa Nui* offers ocean-view rooms and excellent guided excursions.

Eat: Book a table at *Te Moai Sunset* and order the extremely fresh *ceviche*, served with a side of Pacific views.

Drink: Linger after dinner at *Te Moai* to catch the most spectacular sunsets on the island.

The Moai-littered Ahu Tongariki

F

FEZ, MOROCCO

SHOESTRING It's only wandering feet and donkey hooves that tramp across the pedestrianised Fez medina, a Unesco-protected labyrinth of twisting alleys and wardrobe-sized workshops. Market sellers lure passers-by with eye-catching displays of everything from Fassi yellow *babouche* (leather slippers) to finely etched brass mirrors and handloomed *boucherouite* carpets, while the aroma of *bessara* (dried broad bean soup) reveals the location of tucked-away eateries. A more potent scent will guide you to Chouara Tanneries, where workers dip hides into an oversized painter's palette of stone vats filled with colourful dyes.

Stay: Escape the crowds at *Funky Fes*, a mellow hostel south of the medina.

Eat: Fes el Bali and Fes el Jedid are packed with street-food stalls, while *Thami's* is the place to go for simple but satisfying eats like *kefta tajine*.

Drink: As with most Moroccan medinas, drinking is restricted to hotels and riads.

The ornate Bab Bou Jeloud gate in Fes el Bali

Traditional Moroccan mint tea is refreshing in the heat

Colourful dyes of Chouara Tanneries

The medina is packed with dinky stalls

Port city Horta has a rich maritime history

The Atlantic swirling around Azores is home to 24 whale species

Faial is ripe for a road trip

Vulcão dos Capelinhos is a hiking hotspot

FAIAL, PORTUGAL

SAVE A cluster of emerald specks in the mid-Atlantic, the remote Azores has long been a rest stop for transatlantic sailors. A rich maritime tradition lives on in Faial, particularly in the port city of Horta, where passing sailors still leave a painting when they dock – legend has it that paintings ward off bad luck at sea. Head west to discover the island's fiery alter-ego: lush hills give way to barren landscapes sculpted by volcanic cones and lava flows. Intrepid types can hike Vulcão dos Capelinhos, the last volcano to erupt in the Azores in 1958, or sign up for canyoning, rappelling or whale-watching – the surrounding waters are home to 24 species.

Stay: *Pousada Forte da Horta* is a sixteenth-century fort and national monument, with well-preserved crenels and fine views of Mount Pico.

Eat: Overlooking the bay at Porto Pim, *Genuíno* is the brainchild of Genuíno Madruga, the first Portuguese sailor to circumnavigate the globe solo. Try the *almôndegas de atum* (tuna meatballs with a sweet potato purée).

Drink: Knock back a gin while watching live music at the *Oceanic Café*, a popular addition to Horta's cultural scene.

Brunelleschi's Duomo pokes above the skyline

FLORENCE, ITALY

SPLURGE The birthplace of the Renaissance, Florence is Italy's greatest city of art. Museums displaying masterpieces by Michelangelo, Botticelli and Da Vinci line cobbled lanes opening onto charming squares with frescoed churches – don't miss Brunelleschi's Duomo. There's certainly no shortage of cultural delights here – Florence has the highest concentration of artworks anywhere in the world – although the city's culinary scene is equally punchy, with a clutch of superb restaurants. If you want to stay in the heart of the action, book a room at *The Place Firenze* on Piazza di Santa Maria Novella. This hotel actively supports local craftsmanship with The Place of Wonders, a project offering visits to the workshops of artisans, curators and artists.

Stay: *Villa San Michele, a Belmond Hotel* is cut into the forested flanks of the Fiesole hills and offers wide views over Florence's red-tiled rooftops.

Eat: Possibly the prettiest café in Florence, *Cibrèo Trattoria* opened in 1989, though the wood-panelled interior looks at least two hundred years older.

Drink: Inventive cocktails in moody surroundings are in order at *Il Locale*, a newcomer on the much-coveted World's 50 Best Bars hotlist for 2022.

The iconic *David* by Michelangelo

Villa San Michele, a Belmond Hotel

Ponte Vecchio is peppered with small shops

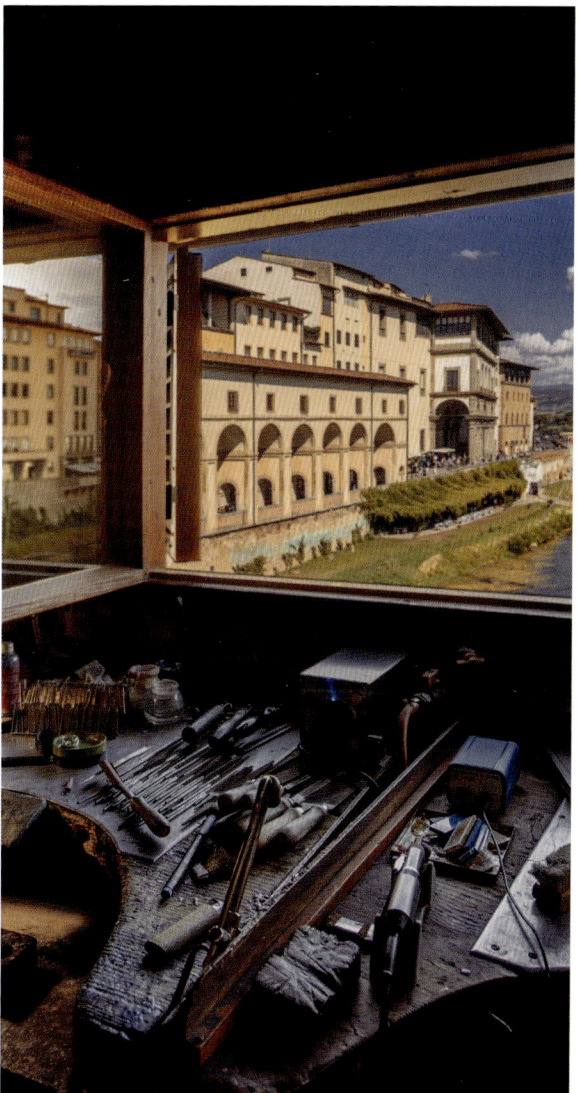

Fratelli Piccini workshop on Ponte Vecchio

G

Gravensteen, castle of the counts

Belgian beer tastings

The narrow cobbled streets of Ghent

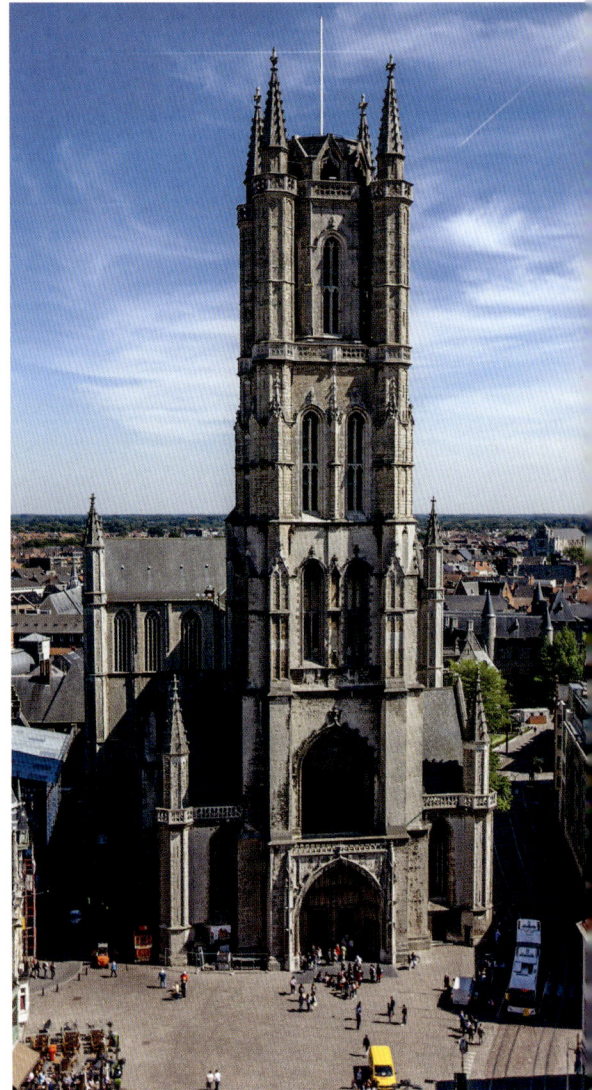
Gothic facade of St Bavo's Cathedral

GHENT, BELGIUM

SHOESTRING Bypass Flemish favourite Bruges in favour of lesser-visited Ghent for the same beautiful canals and medieval architecture – without the crowds. The largest town in Western Europe in the thirteenth and fourteenth centuries, Ghent is a lively university town with a spirited nightlife and a spectacular twelfth-century castle (now a chilling torture museum). Get lost in the cobbled streets lining the canalside to stumble across local bars and shops, before ducking into the Gothic St Bavo's Cathedral to see the *Adoration of the Mystic Lamb*, an early fifteenth-century masterpiece by brothers Hubert and Jan van Eyck. Over ten days in July, Ghent transforms into a 24-hour party city as it pulsates with live music for the Gentse Feesten.

Stay: The *13 O'Clock*, *De Draecke* and *Uppelink* hostels are all easy on the wallet.

Eat: Ghent's cheaper food options cluster around the Korenmarkt; a good option is *Parnassus*, set inside a former Franciscan church.

Drink: *'t Dreupelkot*, the city's last traditional jenever bar, stocks over 215 flavours, while *Folklore* is one of Ghent's few remaining brown cafés.

The Zaha Hadid-designed Riverside Museum

GLASGOW, SCOTLAND

SAVE Drive an hour west of Edinburgh to discover the capital's biggest rival: Glasgow, with its rich cultural life and emerging culinary scene. It hasn't always been this way. A former industrial giant, Glasgow reinvented itself to become a European City of Culture in 1990. It is home to some of Britain's most innovative museums and galleries – Kelvingrove Art Gallery and Museum and the Zaha Hadid-designed Riverside Museum among them – nearly all of which are free. The streets are peppered with Art Nouveau gems by local luminary Charles Rennie Mackintosh, such as *Mackintosh at the Willow*, Scotland Street School Museum and The Lighthouse, now home to the excellent Mackintosh Interpretation Centre. The old shipyards of the Clyde have also been reimagined, particularly in the futuristic spaceship-style Glasgow Science Centre.

Stay: Check out the characterful *Alamo Guest House*; pub-with-rooms *Babbity Bowster*; or *Glasgow Youth Hostel*, set on a grand West End terrace.

Eat: For decent eats in Britain's curry capital, beeline for the *Wee Curry Shop*.

Drink: Embark on a pub crawl through the West End or delve into the edgier nightlife around Glasgow Green.

Mackintosh at the Willow, the brainchild of Charles Rennie Mackintosh

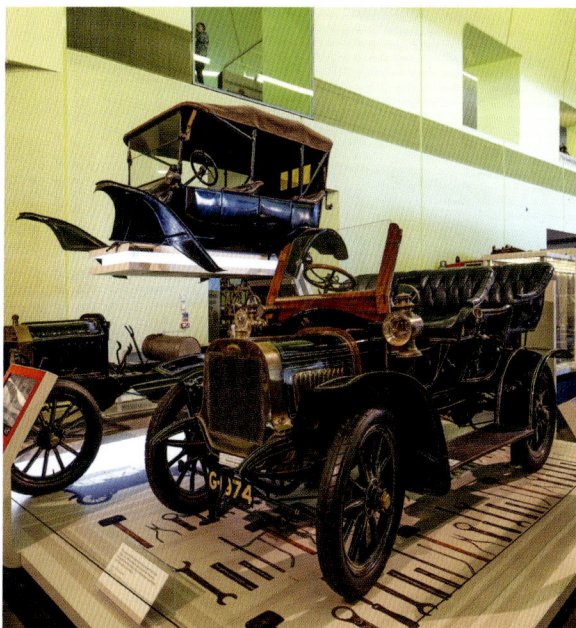

The Riverside Museum traces the history of transport

Glasgow Science Centre

Spitfire Hall, Kelvingrove Art Gallery and Museum

Great Sphinx of Giza

Downtown Cairo is a hub of local life

Museum of Egyptian Antiquities

Great Pyramid of Giza

Barbecued seafood is a staple

GIZA, EGYPT

SPLURGE After a decade of upheaval, a far more hopeful period is afoot in Egypt. In 2022, Egypt hosted COP27, the United Nations Climate Change Conference, while the much-delayed Grand Egyptian Museum is set to open in Giza in 2023. Pegged to be the largest archaeological museum in the world, the space will contain priceless items, including all objects excavated from Tutankhamun's tomb. While in the region, it'd be remiss not to visit the Pyramids, the last remaining wonder of the ancient world. Most visitors hotfoot it to the Great Pyramid of Giza, the Pyramid of Khafre, the Pyramid of Menkaure and the Great Sphinx, but venture further afield to discover lesser-visited tombs, temple ruins and smaller pyramids.

Stay: If money is no object, splash out on an ultra-luxe stay at the *Four Seasons Hotel Cairo at Nile Plaza*.

Eat: Destination restaurants galore await in Cairo; top of the list is *Tamarai*, helmed by a Michelin-starred chef.

Drink: *Cairo Jazz Club* is the place to go for live music, while *Pier 88* has a fun after-hours vibe.

H

Ban Gioc waterfall in Cao Bang

HILL COUNTRY, VIETNAM

SHOESTRING Northern Vietnam's Hill Country is an undulating expanse of shapely mountains contoured by neatly tiered rice terraces and forested crowns. Traditional villages, tucked into the folds of emerald-green hills, are inhabited by some of the nation's 54 ethnic groups. Fortunately for budget travellers, the best way to experience the limestone towers and paddy fields that glint in the morning sun, is on foot. A network of hiking trails connects the hill villages, making for excellent single- and multi-day treks. One of our favourite hiking routes in the region is the Cao Bang trail, which throws waterfalls, caves, hill villages and dramatic mountain vistas at you in quick succession.

Stay: As much for a flashpacker as a backpacker, *White Lotus* is one of the best shoestring options in Sa Pa, the capital of the Hill Country region.

Eat: For memorable budget eats, grab a barbecued kebab from Sa Pa's bustling Am Thuc food court.

Drink: Easily the most authentic drinking experience – whether alcoholic or not – in Vietnam's Hill Country is sitting down with the locals in a makeshift village bar-café.

Banh cuon (rolled rice pancakes)

Traditional costume of the Tày people

Thien Vien Truc Lam Ban Gioc pagoda in Cao Bang

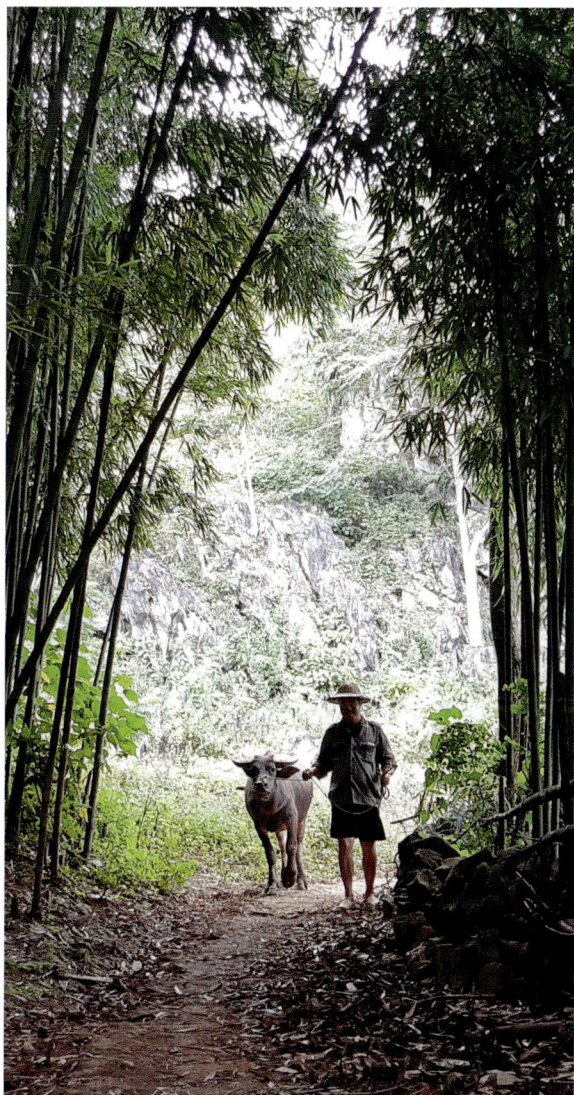

Hill Country has a rural way of life

HVAR, CROATIA

SAVE Of the thousand or so islands in Croatia's glittering archipelago, few match Hvar for its heady combination of bijou towns, pristine beaches, natural beauty and superlative nightlife. Long lauded as the most glamorous island on the Croatian Adriatic, Hvar has a tally of high-end hotels to match; however, there are plenty of ways to enjoy a trip here without blowing your budget. Look for rooms (*sobe*) or apartments rather than hotels – and avoid July and August when prices soar. Take advantage of the decent bus service rather than hire a car, and rent bikes to explore the Unesco-listed Stari Grad Plain. Be sure to hike to the island's highest peak, Sv Nikola – on a clear day you can see all the way to Italy.

Stay: Consider staying in Stari Grad or Vrboska instead of Hvar Town, or book a simple beach hut at the *Cast Away* eco-resort near Zavala.

Eat: If you're ordering seafood, go for mackerel; it's cheaper and more sustainable.

Drink: Buy wine direct from vineyards for a much lower price tag.

Hvar Town, the island's main hub

A traditional Croatian dish of artichoke and chickpeas

Stari Grad, a cheaper alternative to Hvar Town

Pakleni Islands, tiny specks off Hvar's southwest coast

Tai O fishing village

Big Buddha at Po Lin Monastery

Ngong Ping 360 cable car

Lai Ching Heen serves inventive Cantonese cuisine

HONG KONG, CHINA

SPLURGE Dynamic Hong Kong is one of the most vibrant cities in Asia. Its markets crackle with energy, such as the well-loved Nelson Street Wet Market which is peppered with food stalls and where you can discover interesting finds such as thousand-year-old eggs. Take in the waterfront scenery at Victoria Harbour and then scramble up to Victoria Peak for sprawling views of the city below, best seen at sunset. The Sky100 observation deck is another place for incredible vistas. Hop on the Ngong Ping 360 cable car to zip above the skyscrapers to Ngong Ping. From here, you can easily reach Tai O fishing village, Po Lin Monastery and Tian Tan Buddha (Big Buddha).

Stay: Splash out on a luxurious stay at *Mandarin Oriental*, with its antique-filled rooms and tasteful lounges adorned with eighteenth-century Chinese textiles.

Eat: *Lai Ching Heen* is one of Hong Kong's best restaurants for cutting-edge Cantonese cooking – and for the excellent service and harbour views.

Drink: Single malt fan? *Club Qing* is a smart bar specialising in Japanese whisky (it claims to carry every available variety) plus rare Scotch – tasting sets are available.

View of Hong Kong from Braemar Hill

View of Islamabad from the Margalla Hills

ISLAMABAD, PAKISTAN

SHOESTRING Though Pakistan struggles to shake off its reputation as a dangerous country, most of its cities and northern areas are not only safe to visit but absolutely stunning to boot. Islamabad is a perfect entry point, sitting next to one of the country's main airports and sheltered by the ash-grey Margalla Hills — a teaser of the Karakoram range further north. Pakistan's capital was planned in the 1960s by a Greek architect with a vision to create a forest-clad city unlike any other in South Asia. Its grid structure, with large and clean avenues, feels very different from the adjacent twin city of Rawalpindi, whose urban chaos resembles Lahore and Karachi. But in Islamabad, shopping malls rub shoulders with teahouses and open-air restaurants, testifying to one of the most progressive faces of Pakistan. The Faisal Mosque dominates the city's skyline, and is a glorious spot at sunset.

Stay: Bunk at *Backpackers Islamabad* in the Mehr-E colony of District E-11, a friendly hostel that offers guided tours to Gilgit-Baltistan.

Eat: Dine with a view at the popular ridge-hanging *Monal* restaurant.

Drink: Swing by *Chaiwala* in E Block Park, run by famed chai-maker and social media star Arshad Khan, for a cup of soul-nourishing goodness.

Supreme Court of Pakistan

Opulent interiors of Faisal Mosque

Pakistan Monument and heritage museum

The Faisal Mosque is one of the largest in Asia

Inverness unfurls from the banks of the River Ness

Black Isle Brewery is famed for its organic craft beer

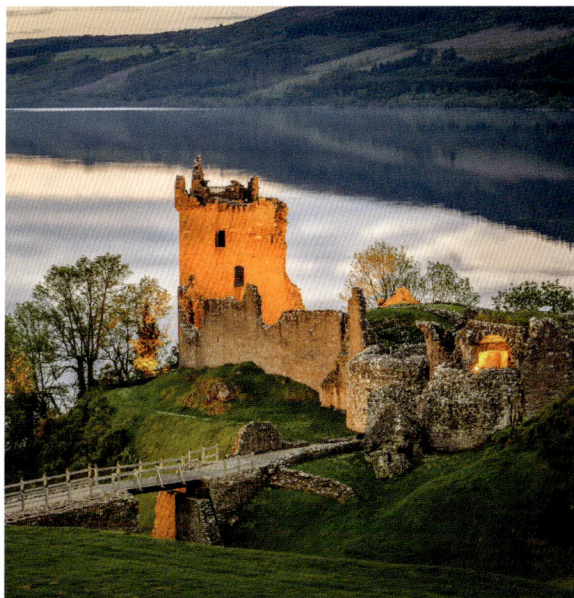

Black Isle Brewery is located north of Inverness

Inverness Castle is currently undergoing a huge revamp

Expect sea-to-plate cuisine in Inverness

INVERNESS, SCOTLAND

SAVE Inverness is a history lesson of a city. It might lack the showy nature of Edinburgh or Glasgow, yet it hums with a quiet energy that gets under your skin. Its hard-working global appeal nods to the proximity of Loch Ness, but more recently the city has registered as the start and end point for the 830km-long North Coast 500 — Scotland's take on America's Route 66. The city itself is worth at least 48 hours of your time, though. Highlights include Inverness Museum and Art Gallery, the river walk to the Ness Islands, and Inverness Castle, a red-sandstone bastion undergoing a huge revamp (reopens in 2025).

Stay: On a pretty stretch of the River Ness, *Glenmoriston Townhouse Hotel* shelters a sublime restaurant and whisky bar, with 260 top-shelf drams.

Eat: Pick from locally sourced seafood, venison and rump steak at *The Mustard Seed*, served with river views.

Drink: *Black Isle Bar & Rooms* is the Inverness outpost of the eponymous brewery, beloved for its organic craft beer.

The Throne Room in the harem at Topkapi Palace

Four Seasons Hotel Istanbul at Sultanahmet

The Grand Bazaar, one of the world's oldest covered markets

Topkapi Palace looms above the Marmara Sea

ISTANBUL, TURKEY

SPLURGE Istanbul is a magnetising city where West and East collide to glorious effect. Against a minaret-studded skyline, a jumble of imposing architecture jostles for attention. The opulent Topkapi Palace offers a glimpse into the lives of Ottoman sultans, while the cascading domes of the Blue Mosque sashay before Sultanahmet Park. Piece together the history of the city through the Hagia Sophia Grand Mosque, its mix of Byzantine opulence and Ottoman grandeur nodding to the various empires in power throughout the years. Close by, the Grand Bazaar is one of the largest covered markets in the world, with over four thousand stalls packed into sixty streets. For the finest city views, sign up for a luxury cruise to glide down the Bosphorus.

Stay: The *Four Seasons Hotel Istanbul at Sultanahmet* is unrivalled for luxury: rooms are palatial, the Neoclassical architecture is splendid, the spa divine.

Eat: Rooftop restaurant *Mikla* has sensational views over the old city and Bosphorus as well as excellent food – Turkish with a Scandinavian twist.

Drink: *Leb-i-Derya* is an upmarket bar in Beyoğlu, with Bosphorus views.

J

Larch-lined hiking trails wend through the Julian Alps

Ibex cling to mountainsides

The Julian Alps are contoured by saw-tooth peaks

Paddleboarding in the Great Soča Gorge

JULIAN ALPS, SLOVENIA

SHOESTRING The Julian Alps are one of the most stunningly beautiful mountain ranges in Europe – a great sprawl of jagged limestone peaks slashed by deep river valleys and gorges, and studded with jewel-like lakes. Around two-thirds of the Julian Alps lie in Slovenia, with the remainder marching over the border into Italy – most of the Slovenian part is protected as part of the 880 sq km Triglav National Park. Their biodiversity is extraordinary – from ibex to golden eagles and brown bear, and masses of wildflowers. It's here that you'll find Slovenia's highest mountain: the awe-inspiring 2864m Mt Triglav – but don't just restrict your focus to Triglav. There are plenty of other amazing places to see: the emerald-green River Soča is great for kayaking adventures, while the Juliana Trail is a scenic 270km circuit skirting Lake Bled and lesser-visited sibling Bohinj.

Stay: Plenty of wonderful farmsteads and guesthouses, along with a few campsites, cater to budget travellers.

Eat: Most accommodation offers local, seasonal cuisine.

Drink: Oenophiles should opt for the extended Juliana Trail, with an add-on that nudges into wine country.

The Juliana Trail skirts Lake Bled

Saucy sculptures abound at Love Land

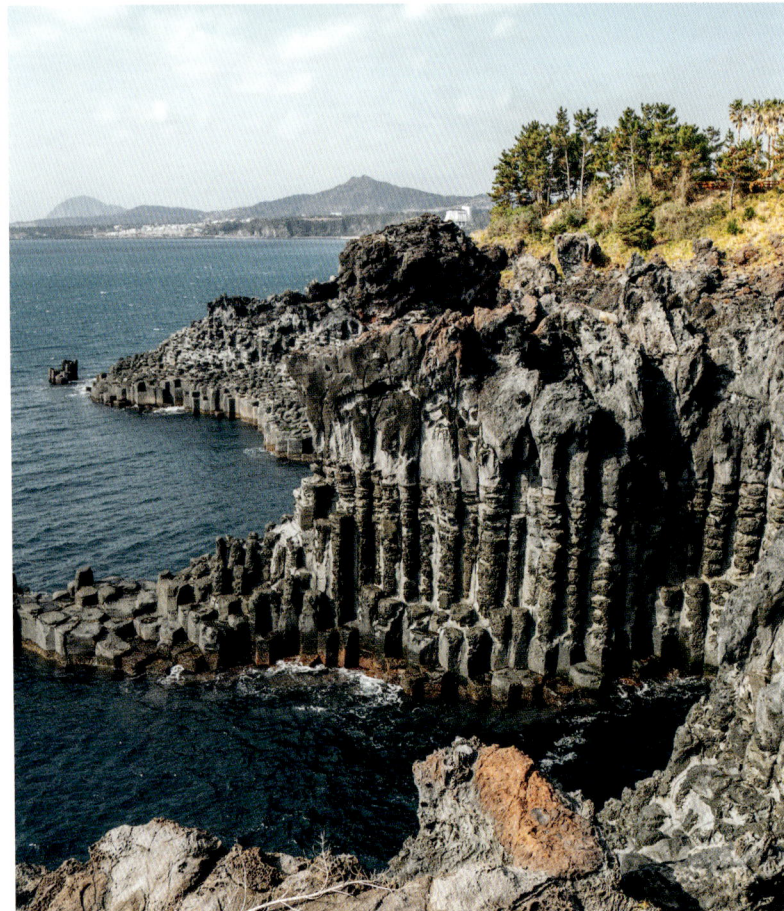

Haenyeo (female freedivers) off Udo

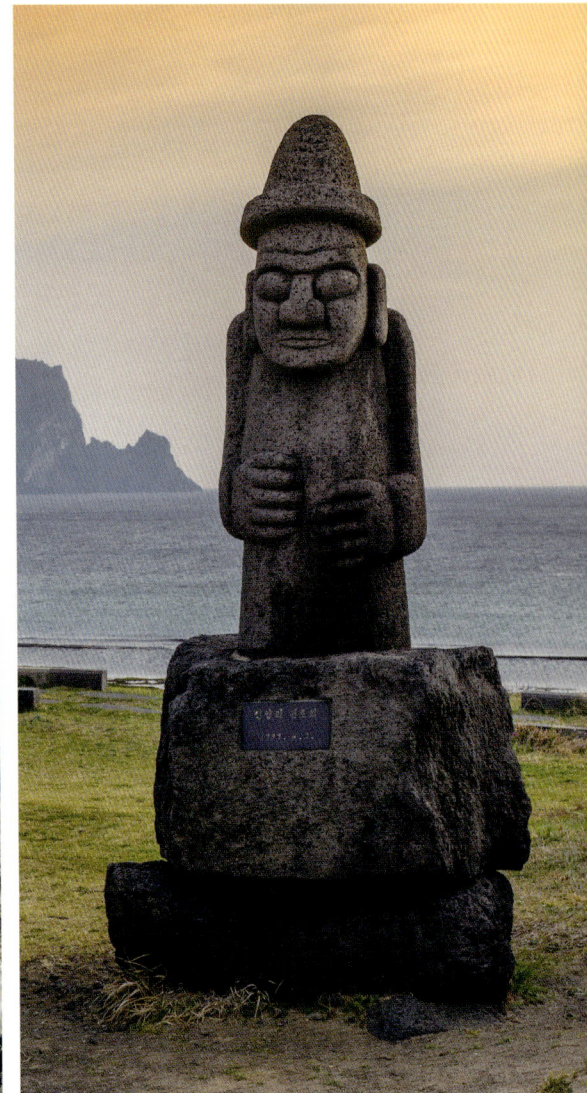

The cathedral-like cliffs of Jusangjeolli-dae

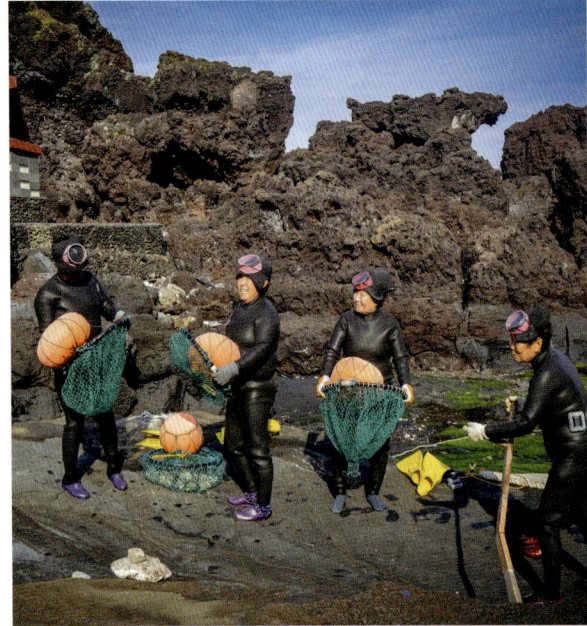

The origins of _hareubang_ statues are unknown

JEJU-DO, SOUTH KOREA

SAVE On the forested island of Jeju-do, history and folk tales mingle freely. You can see the revered *haenyeo* (female freedivers) disappearing beneath the waves off Udo islet; admire traditional volcanic-rock houses; and spot mysterious *hareubang* statues, their origins unknown. Keeping watch over it all is Hallasan – at 1947m, South Korea's highest point. Hike to the cloud--shrouded summit, or for a less strenuous look at the island's volcanic past, visit Sangumburi crater, the geometric cliffs of Jusangjeolli-dae, or the eerie Manjanggul lava tubes. Culture abounds at the Jeju Museum of Art, Sanbaggulsa Cave Temple, and the Jeju and Seong-eup folk villages - or check out Love Land, a playful sculpture park with an eyebrow-raising theme.

Stay: *LOTTE City Hotel* has a great central Jeju City location and a rooftop pool. In southern Jeju, *Hotel Seogwipean* has panoramic ocean views.

Eat: Explore the street-food stalls of Jeju City's Dongmun Market, or the smaller but less crowded Seomun Market.

Drink: Try Jeju's specialist tipple, Omegi Malgeun-sul, at Jeju Island Brewery.

Spiky trees and bulbous boulders on the Cap Rock Trail

JOSHUA TREE, USA

SPLURGE Ask any Los Angeles hipster where best to rekindle the bohemian spirit of the 1960s and many will give the same answer: Joshua Tree. Fixated by the pull of the high desert, moneyed travellers now take trips to the park to be inspired by its light and shadow, to stay up late and watch the sunrise, and to free-climb the outcrops of Cap Rock. This is a place of rock 'n' roll pilgrimages, too. Listen to Wild Horses by *The Rolling Stones* or to U2's *The Joshua Tree* resonate around the bars and boutiques along 29 Palms Highway, or go all out at Coachella Valley Music and Arts Festival in April.

Stay: Opened in 1950, *Joshua Tree Inn* is a fabled hacienda and pilgrimage site for music fans. Donovan and Emmylou Harris stayed here to zone out, while former Byrd and Rolling Stones' cohort Gram Parsons died from an overdose in room number 8 in 1973.

Eat: Roadhouse burger stops are a dime a dozen on the 29 Palms Highway — *Natural Sisters Café* is the antidote, with its organic, vegan menu.

Drink: *Pappy and Harriet's* is a high-desert saloon and live music venue; past acts include Arctic Monkeys, Vampire Weekend and Sir Paul McCartney.

Wind-sculpted desertscapes

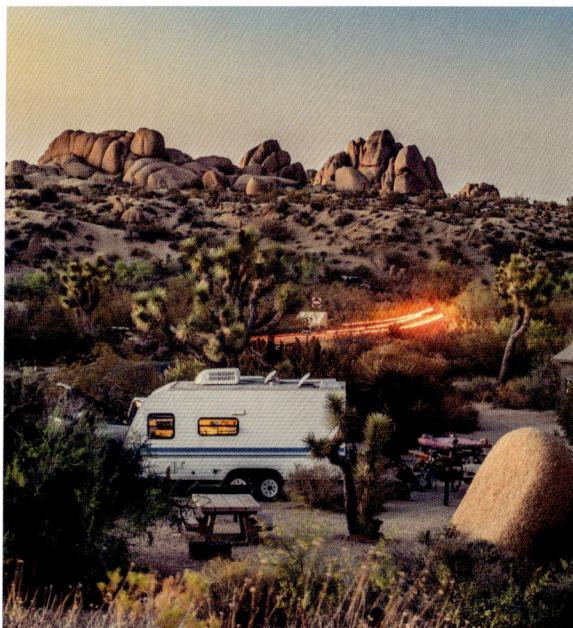
The rock formations glow at sunset

Mark Dutton, formerly of Chris Robinson Brotherhood, at *Pappy and Harriet's*

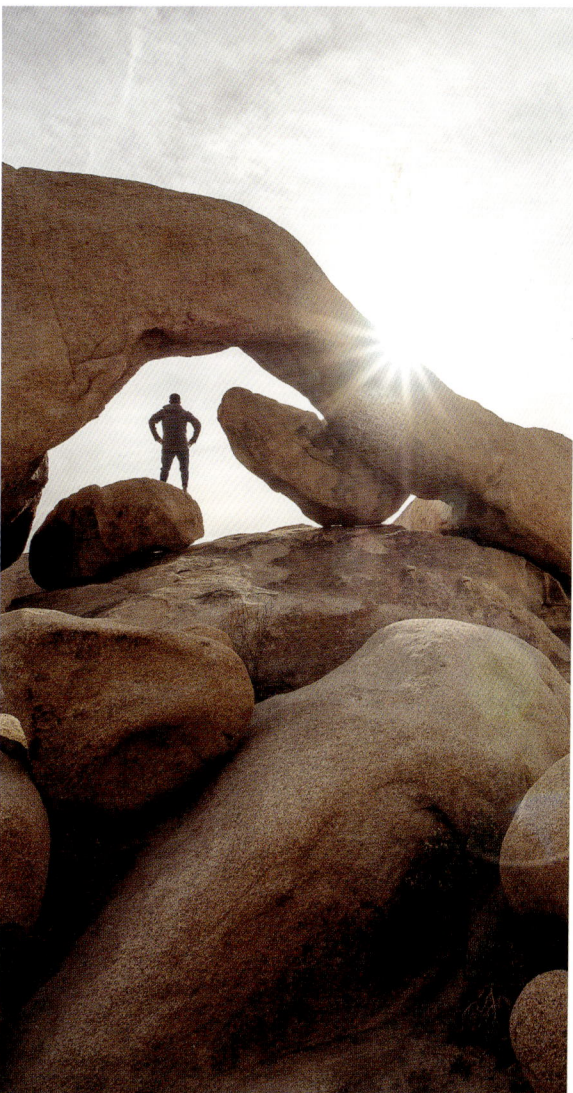
Arch Rock at Joshua Tree National Park

K

Bhaktapur, a Unesco-listed city in Kathmandu Valley

Swayambhunath, or Monkey Temple

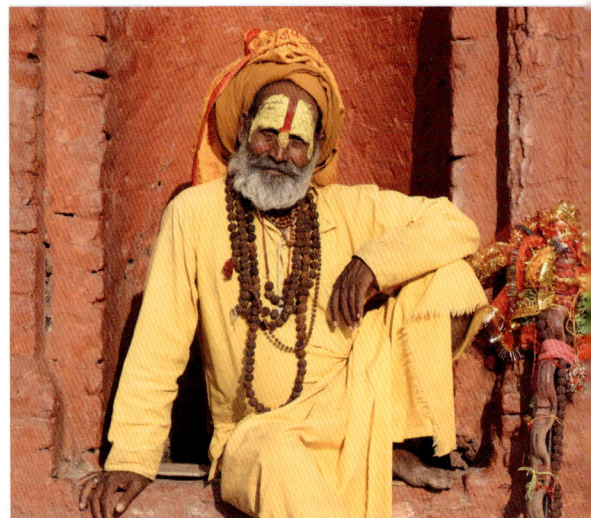
Bustling street near Durbar Square

Sadhu (holy person) at Pashupatinath Temple

KATHMANDU, NEPAL

SHOESTRING The gateway to the Himalayas, Kathmandu is guarded by the Earth's tallest peaks: the Everest-famed Solukhumbu range, visible from the capital's rooftops on a clear day. So, no wonder the city's tourist-driven neighbourhood of Thamel booms with narrow shops bulging to the rafters with outdoor gear. If you're in the market for hiking equipment, prices are always at least a smidgen manoeuvrable. Hindu and Buddhist cultures permeate everyday life, with the pageantry of each festival bringing its own entertainment. The vast hilltop temple of Swayambhunath (or Monkey Temple, for the macaques who've laid claim to it) costs just a pound's entrance. Pay locals' prices at hole-in-the-wall cafés, often run by matriarchs, where a casual greeting of namaste, didi (hello, older sister) will help you fit right in.

Stay: Budget travellers book into Thamel's hostels, such as the *Shangri-La Boutique Hotel*. Just off Paknajo Street, a cluster of simple guesthouses offers cheap private en suites.

Eat: *Dal bhat* (a platter of rice, lentil soup, vegetables and pickles) is always best value as seconds come free. Join the locals at *Muktinath Thakali Kitchen* in Thamel.

Drink: Live-music bars are the staple of Nepalese nightlife: *Purple Haze* offers free entry most nights. For cut-price coffee and bohemian nostalgia, try Freak Street's *Snowman Cafe*.

Boudhanath Stupa

KUCHING, MALAYSIA

SAVE Once as unhurried as the meandering river that bisects it, Kuching – the capital of Sarawak in Malaysian Borneo – has shifted up a few gears in recent years. Buzzing bars rub walls with chic hostels, noodle bars and cafés in Carpenter Street – one central, irresistible lane that mixes modernity with colonial and Indigenous histories. Even the vestiges of the White Rajahs, who ruled the state between 1841 and 1946, have caught up with modernity. Across the river from the Old Court House is Fort Margherita, now housing the Brooke Gallery, and the Borneo Cultures Museum. Outside town is Semenggoh Wildlife Centre, which rehabilitates orphaned orangutans, and the Bako and Gunung Gading national parks, the latter home to the world's largest flower – the foul-smelling rafflesia.

Stay: Bed down at *Ranee*, a nineteenth-century shophouse turned boutique hotel.

Eat: Devour lava cakes at *Commons*, where political decisions were once made.

Drink: Have a drink with a conscience at *Monkee Bar*, where half of all profits support orangutan conservation at Semenggoh Wildlife Centre.

Kuching Esplanade is a pretty spot at sunset

Indian Mosque, the oldest in Kuching (1863)

Fort Margherita was built in 1879 by Charles Brooke, Rajah of Sarawak

Carpenter Street is a playful enclave in central Kuching

The Bob Marley Museum is set in the iconic musician's former home

Rastafari has roots in 1930s Jamaica

The cloud-raking Blue Mountains

Fort Charles in Port Royal

KINGSTON, JAMAICA

SPLURGE A trip to Jamaica is incomplete without a stop in Kingston, the birthplace of reggae and dancehall. The streets come alive during Carnival when revellers in extravagantly feathered and beaded costumes dance to soca's infectious rhythms. Slip down a beat in the Blue Mountains with a coffee-farm tour or scenic bike ride before a farm-to-table culinary experience at *EITS Café*. For a different perspective, splash out on a helicopter tour or board a yacht from Port Royal to Lime or Maiden Cay to skim through jewelled waters.

Stay: The *AC Hotel by Marriott* overlooks the Bob Marley Museum and National Gallery in town, while *Strawberry Hill* is cradled among the Blue Mountains.

Eat: Fine restaurants, such as *Broken Plate*, *Annex East Japanese* and *Uncorked*, are wedged between local cookery shops. Sunken former pirate haven Port Royal is the best spot for seafood; pick of the bunch is *Gloria's*.

Drink: Kingston's effervescent spirit pulsates after dark; some of the best after-hours hangouts include *Janga's Soundbar*, *Dub Club* and *CRU*.

Badacsony is a fine wine region

LAKE BALATON, HUNGARY

SHOESTRING Swerve tourist heavyweight Budapest and head west to discover Lake Balaton – the largest in Central Europe. This huge freshwater pool offers plenty of opportunities for visitors. Wallow in the bathwater-warm shallows of Lake Héviz – the biggest swimmable thermal lake in the world (New Zealand's Frying Pan Lake is too hot to dip a toe in) – on the western fringes of Balaton. Travel north for wine tours and tastings in vine-combed Badacsony or sun and surf in wind-tousled Szigliget. The eastern shores of Balaton lure electronic music fans to Balaton Sound, a popular festival that attracts big names like David Guetta and The Chainsmokers.

Stay: Bargain stays abound in Lake Balaton: try family-run *Kaméleon Hostel* in Balatongyörökön; *Vadkacsa Étterem és Panzió* with its own private beach in Balatonkenese; or *Villa Kabala* in Szigliget for its excellent restaurant.

Eat: *Baricska Csárda* in Balatonfüred serves Hungarian classics to diners beneath vine-entwined trellises; the paprika-spiked catfish is divine.

Drink: *Cocktail Terrace* in Balatonfenyves is a buzzy spot for alfresco drinks, while *Cafe Kamilla* in Fonyód flaunts the finest lake views around.

Lake Hévíz, the world's largest swimmable thermal lake

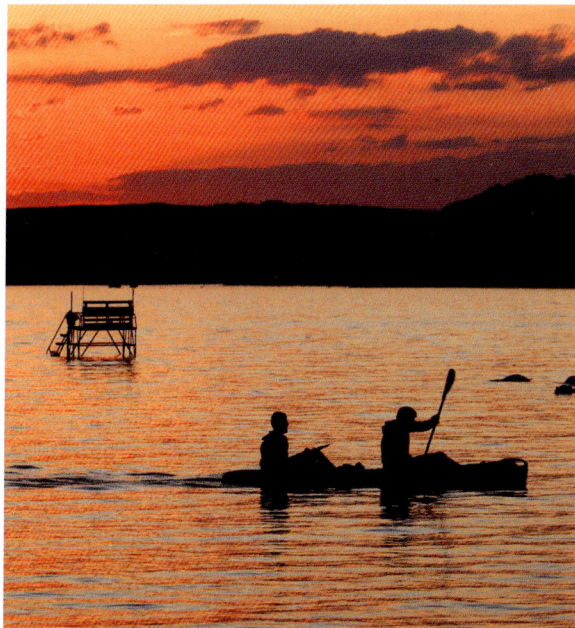

Lake Balaton, best explored by kayak

zigliget Castle dates back to 1260

Tihany Abbey watches over the boat-peppered lake

Lalibela is a sacred site for Ethiopian Orthodox Christians

The Lasta Mountains conceal the hidden churches

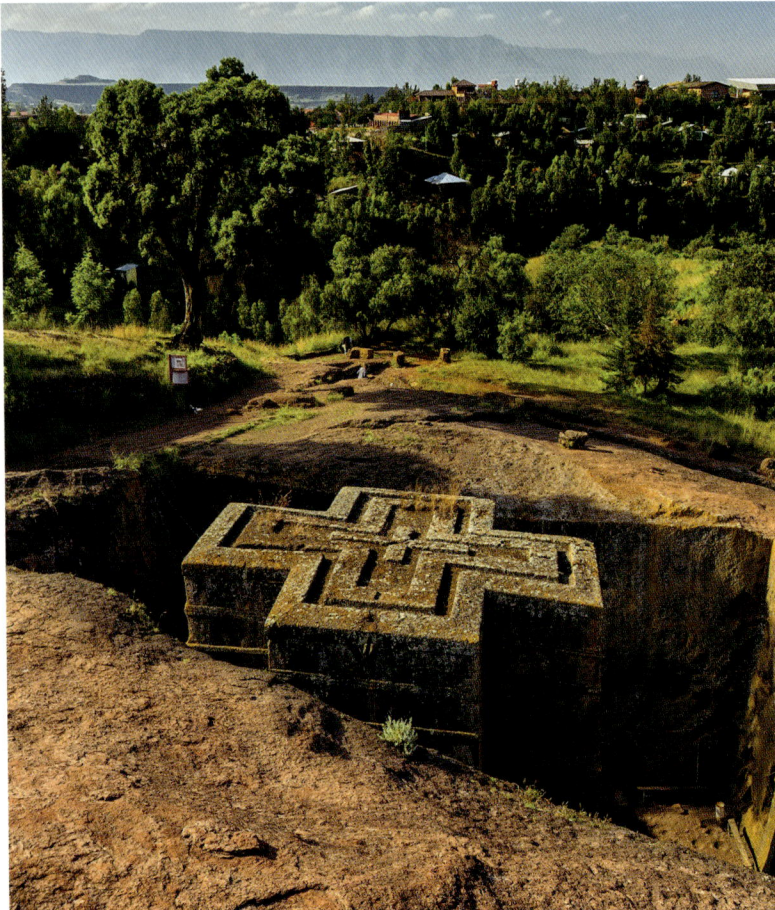

The Church of St George is carved in the shape of a cross

Interiors are adorned with sculptures

LALIBELA, ETHIOPIA

SAVE The rock-hewn churches of Lalibela are among the most impressive Christian monuments in Africa. Thought to date back to the twelfth century, these monolithic edifices are attributed to the medieval Ethiopian king Gebre Meskel, who – according to legend – saw a vision of Jerusalem in a dream, and determined to build a new holy city in his own kingdom. And a mighty fine vision it turned out: eleven churches, all carved beneath ground, connected by a maze of passages. The most impressive, the Church of St George, is sculpted in the shape of a cross. The interiors are just as staggering, many etched with intricate decorations; book a guided tour for a glimpse inside.

Stay: Pick *Sora Lodge* for fantastic views of the rocky valleys from its terrace.

Eat: The table to book is at the architecturally remarkable *Ben Abeba* restaurant, which serves up delicious Ethiopian–Scottish fusion meals.

Drink: Ethiopian coffee is up there with the best in the world: follow your nose to the scent of freshly roasted beans to find local cafés.

San Pedro Church on Plaza de Armas

A treasure trove awaits at the Gold Museum

Chef Pía León creates inventive Peruvian dishes at *Kjolle*

Hotel B in Barranco

Huaca Pucllana, a pre-Inca pyramid in Miraflores

LIMA, PERU

SPLURGE Lima might not be the prettiest of capitals, but what this Pacific coast city lacks in aesthetics, it makes up for in flavour. The foodie hub of South America, Lima is packed with restaurants to meet all budgets, but where it excels is fine dining. Work up an appetite wandering the saffron-hued colonial buildings in the old town, starting with the Plaza de Armas; for an architectural contrast, visit the pre-Inca temple Huaca Pucllana in the Miraflores district.

Loop around the city's excellent museums to further understand Peru's complex past: the National Museum of Archaeology, Anthropology and History is a perfect introduction; the Larco Museum is famed for its collection of erotic art; while the dazzling Gold Museum shares the country's rich heritage.

Stay: Rest your head at stylish *Hotel B* in Barranco.

Eat: Indulge in tasting menus at award-winning restaurants *Central*, *Maido*, *Mayta*, *Kjolle* or *Astrid y Gastón*.

Drink: Expect Peruvian twists on classic cocktails at moody-toned *Carnaval*, one of the World's 50 Best Bars.

M

MEDELLÍN, COLOMBIA

SHOESTRING Fun-packed (and often sun-packed) Medellín may be known as the City of Eternal Spring, but Antioquia's capital hasn't always lived through joyful times. Mentioning cartel kingpin Pablo Escobar is obvious but since his demise in 1993, positive progress has been made – especially over the past two decades – in terms of safety and accessibility. For a poignant insight into Colombia's years living under armed conflict, head to the free Casa de la Memoria then visit Comuna 13. Formerly known as the world's most dangerous neighbourhood, today it is full of positive energy and hope. Hop on the city escalators to see street artists and musicians, ride the cable car for an aerial perspective or simply stroll the city to spot the voluminous works of renowned sculptor Botero.

Stay: Consider staying at *Selina*, a hostel created with digital nomads in mind.

Eat: Fill up on Colombian-Asian dishes at *Moshi*; think sushi, ramen and tataki.

Drink: Grab a cup of excellent Antioquia coffee at speciality roastery *Pergamino*.

Comuna 13 is infused with a fresh energy

The Metrocable whisks citygoers up steep hills

Casa de la Memoria

The city is dotted with sculptures by Colombian artist Fernando Botero

Mackie Mayor food hall occupies an 1858 Grade II-listed building

Manchester Art Gallery

Science and Industry Museum

The John Rylands Library shelters the St John Fragment

MANCHESTER, ENGLAND

SAVE With its long-lasting musical legacy, Manchester is one of the best spots in the UK for live tunes. The Northern Quarter resonates with the sound of open-mic nights, jazz evenings and guitar sessions, while tours are geared to every band that's emerged from the city: Oasis, Joy Division, New Order, The Stone Roses, The Smiths. The city isn't short on culture, either: a fine roster of galleries and museums includes the Manchester Art Gallery, The Whitworth, Factory International, Esea Contemporary and the Manchester Jewish Museum. Behind its Victorian neo-Gothic facade, the John Rylands Research Institute and Library shelters the earliest New Testament writing ever found.

Stay: *Motel One* and *ABode* are among the city's plentiful budget chain hotels.

Eat: *Mughli Charcoal* is the main calling card on Manchester's Curry Mile.

Drink: Elbows at the ready, Manchester's smallest pub, the Victorian-era *Circus Tavern*, is a favourite pit stop in the city centre.

Golden-stone buildings tumble down a sheer ravine

MATERA, ITALY

SPLURGE A few years ago, few travellers had heard of Matera. But then the southern Italian city scooped joint European Capital of Culture in 2019 and was a filming location for James Bond movie *No Time To Die* – and now it's creeping onto the radar. The extraordinary city is carved into a rocky outcrop in Basilicata, its huddle of *sassi* (cave dwellings) clinging to the flanks of a sheer ravine. Boutique hotels and restaurants are tucked between frescoed churches and golden-stoned cathedrals in the Unesco-listed old centre. The best way to explore is on foot, especially at sunset when the honey-hued buildings glow. Duck down narrow alleys to stumble across cafés, bars and galleries, and climb zigzagging staircases for ever-changing vistas.

Stay: The room to book is at *Sextantio Le Grotte Della Civita*, a chic bolthole with bare stone walls, pale cobbled floors and beautiful arches.

Eat: Michelin-listed *Baccanti* is set in a beautiful cave complex; try the orecchiette pasta with chicory and fava bean purée.

Drink: *Area 8* is a cool bar with vintage decor that lures a youngish crowd to its live music performances and local DJs.

The ancient *sassi* (cave dwellings)

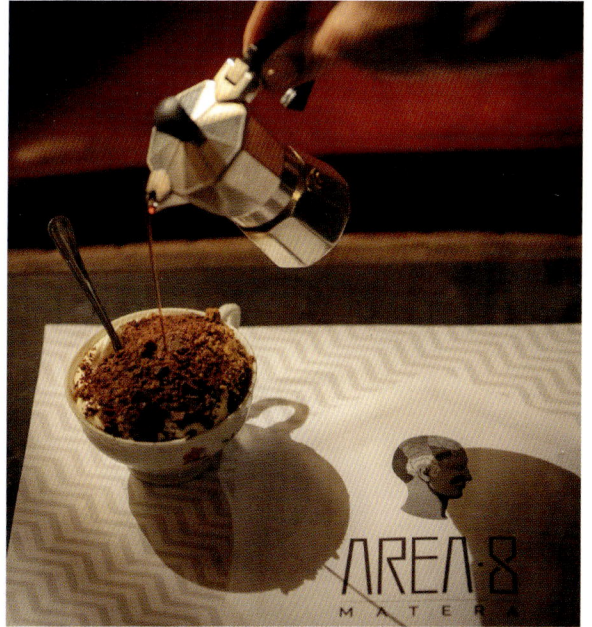

Area 8 is a local hangout

Sextantio *Le Grotte Della Civita* is strung across a series of caves

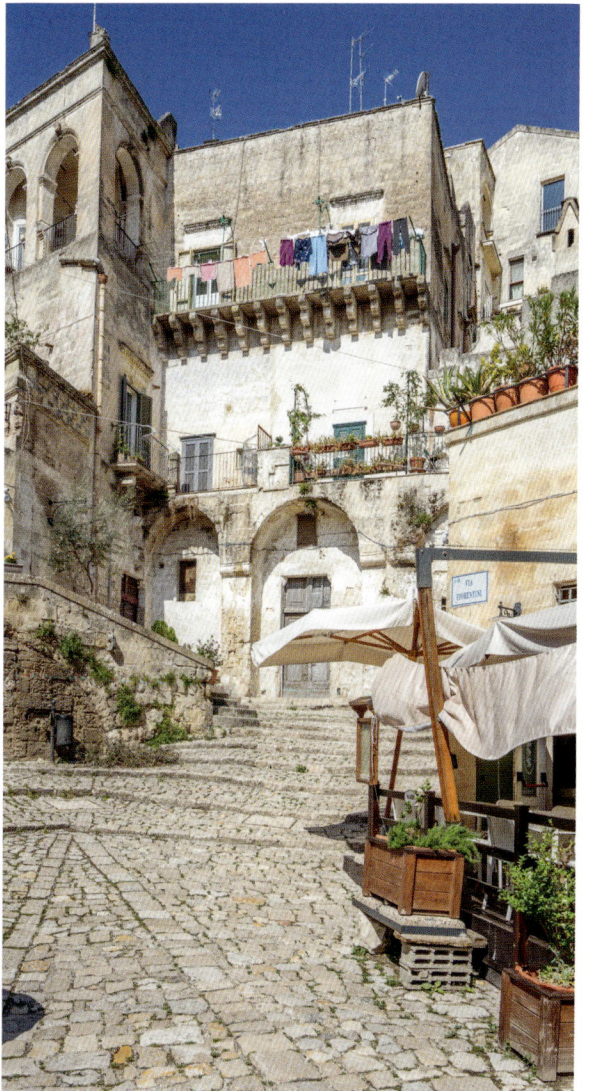

Stone staircases crisscross the city

N

Petrovaradin Fortress: the Gibraltar of the Danube

Freedom Square

EXIT Festival is a four-day extravaganza

Novi Sad is threaded by the Danube River

Hit the road to explore the monasteries of Fruška Gora

NOVI SAD, SERBIA

SHOESTRING An hour's drive north of Belgrade, youthful Novi Sad sits proudly astride the mighty Danube. Serbia's second city has gained a party reputation in recent years thanks to the banging EXIT Festival, a four-day shindig held at the atmospheric Petrovaradin Fortress, a formidable lemon-yellow complex that once stood as a barrier between the Austrians and Turks. The morning after the night before, revellers retreat to the Štrand – a sandy riverside beach lined by open-air cafés and bars. To escape the crowds, head to Fruška Gora National Park, whose low hills are peppered with hiking trails, Orthodox monasteries and vineyards.

Stay: Funky Hostel Sova has a mix of rooms and dorms.

Eat: Follow your nose to the irresistible waft of grilled meat – *ćevapi* and *pljeskavica* – to find local favourites.

Drink: Try a punchy *sljivovica* (plum brandy) at Pivnica Gusan.

Mount Yoshino is planted with around 30,000 cherry trees

NARA, JAPAN

SAVE Nara, just 35km south of Kyoto and 28km east of Osaka, is commonly visited as a day-trip, but linger overnight to discover a quieter side to the city once the crowds leave. Japan's first permanent capital – then called Heijo-kyo, 'Citadel of Peace' – from 710 AD until 794 AD, the city witnessed a glorious period of artistic and architectural creativity. Eight Unesco World Heritage Sites are crammed within Nara's slender boundaries, though the city's most famous attraction is its deer. Once considered the messengers of the gods, these pretty creatures are protected as 'natural monuments'. Follow their clacking hooves from Nara Park to Todaiji Temple, home to the Great Buddha Hall and its whopping 15m-tall Buddha, cast from 500 tonnes of bronze.

Stay: *Guesthouse Nara Backpackers* is set in a handy spot near Kintetsu-Nara Station, while *Guesthouse Tsunoya*, to the south of Naramachi, has capsule-style beds.

Eat: If you visit on the last Sunday of the month, treat yourself to lunch on-the-go from the Nara Foodshed farmers' market. Otherwise, try *Hiyori* for its speciality *yamato-yasai* – the vegetable cuisine of Nara.

Drink: *The Stand* is a fun standing bar with draught beer, shochu and sake.

Nara deer are protected as natural monuments

Daibutsu, or the Great Buddha, in Todaiji Temple

Todaiji Temple conceals a huge 15m-tall Buddha

Sake is the tipple of choice

St Louis Cathedral, the oldest in continuous use in the USA

The *Spotted Cat Music Club* is an intimate jazz venue

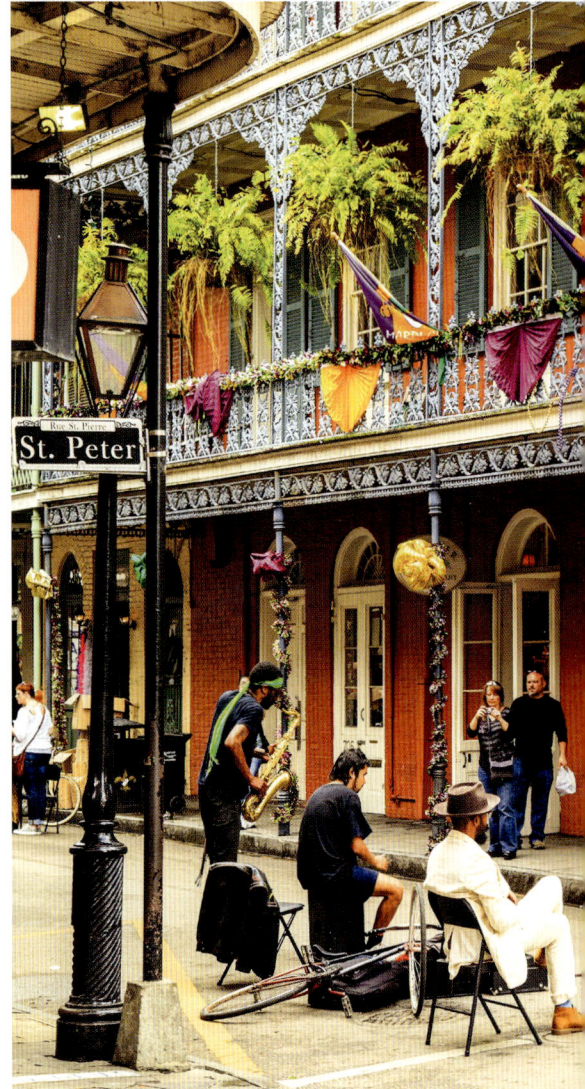

The *Columns* bar is a cosy hangout

Jazz permeates the city

NEW ORLEANS, USA

SPLURGE One of the most intoxicating cities in the Deep South, New Orleans is a rich tapestry of cocktail bars, jazz clubs and design-led hotels. Get lost in the French Quarter, a feast of Creole cottages, chic jewellers and artist studios – Royal Street, with its treasure-filled antique stores and galleries, is a shopping hotspot. Oozing luxury, NOLA's Garden District is all columned mansions and sun-dappled hotel courtyards where you can sink artisan cocktails. For extra indulgence, steal away into *The Ritz-Carlton* for a spa treatment. After dark, *Preservation Hall* is the hottest ticket in town for live jazz.

Stay: The French Quarter's *Hotel Monteleone* offers a masterclass in luxury with its sumptuous suites, literary history and iconic revolving *Carousel Bar*.

Eat: Linger over brunch at *Brennan's*, a fine Creole spot known for inventing the bananas foster dessert, or try *Herbsaint* for French-Southern dishes.

Drink: *Peychaud's*, set in the courtyard of *Hotel Maison de Ville*, is a fine place to sip a Sazerac. Special mention goes to the elegant *Columns* hotel bar too.

O

OHRID, NORTH MACEDONIA

SHOESTRING The most iconic spot in North Macedonia, Lake Ohrid is a 360 sq km blue expanse cradled among snow-streaked mountains and tipping across the border into Albania. The Unesco-listed lake was formed well over a million years ago, from tectonic movement rather than erosion (similar to Siberia's Lake Baikal), and it brims with relict species, some 200 of them found nowhere else on Earth. On its shores, Ohrid town is one of Europe's oldest human settlements. Its cobbled, history-soaked streets cascade down to the waterfront, and are peppered with exquisite medieval churches – it's said the city once had 365 of them, one for each day of the year. Don't miss the clifftop Church of St John at Kaneo or the magnificent Icon Gallery. Nearby, Galičica National Park is superb for hiking.

Stay: For good-value sleeps, try *Ohrid Boutique Apartments* or *Villa Varosh*.

Eat: The lake is flanked by a lovely boardwalk, lined by small restaurants.

Drink: Take your pick from the string of bars tracing the water's edge.

Ohrid town tumbles down to the lake's shores

Boats dock at Ohrid's tiny harbour

Church of St John is thought to date to the thirteenth century

Restaurants pepper Ohrid's streets and lakeside

Fountain-dotted courtyards in the colonial core

San Martín Tilcajete is an artisanal enclave near Oaxaca

Squash blossom quesadillas with Oaxaca cheese

Colonial buildings line the historic centre

OAXACA, MEXICO

SAVE The cosmopolitan capital of the eponymous state, Oaxaca blends colourful markets and exuberant festivals with sophisticated dining, fine hotels and a raucous nightlife. The city's cobbled walkways are lined with artisanal craft stores and local art galleries, and everywhere you look are striking examples of Baroque architecture – where Spanish and Native influences are intermingled to arresting effect. Oaxaca sprawls across the belly of a deep-set valley, 1600m above sea level, yet in the colonial centre just about everything can be easily reached on foot. The cultural (and budget-friendly) highlights of any visit include Museo Tamayo and its excellent contemporary art collection, the Church of Santo Domingo de Guzmán, and the nearby archaeological site of Mitla.

Stay: *Niut-Ja* is a revamped old-style courtyard hotel.

Eat: No-frills *La Red* is the city's best spot for seafood.

Drink: *El Barracuda* draws in the crowds with live music.

Church of Santo Domingo de Guzmán pokes above the skyline

The Deichman Library

The Thief overlooks the Oslofjord

Follow the culinary trail to Mathallen Food Hall

The Munch gallery pays homage to the Norwegian painter

OSLO, NORWAY

SPLURGE Oslo is causing a stir with its exciting new cultural scene. The Munch gallery and National Museum have sprung up alongside the Deichman library, home to the Future Library, a secret archive of unseen works by the likes of Karl Ove Knausgård, Sjón and David Mitchell, to be unsealed and read in 2114. Oslo is firmly on the foodie map thanks to a growing crop of destination restaurants – *Pjoltergeist* and three-starred *Maaemo* among them. Elsewhere, the Mathallen Food Hall is packed to the rafters with street food-style stalls.

Stay: *Hotel Bristol* has genteel 1920s glamour in spades plus wonderfully personable staff and a buffet breakfast to die for, while *The Thief* tops the list for its unbearably stylish rooms, lovely spa and rooftop terrace.

Eat: *Omakase* is a tiny, ten-seat restaurant that's perfected the art of sushi; expect meticulously crafted and totally delicious creations.

Drink: Kick off the evening with an expertly mixed cocktail in retro-cool surroundings at *Internasjonalen* before heading to *Herr Nilsen*, a small and intimate jazz club whose brick walls are decorated with music memorabilia.

P

Sinan Pasha Mosque's minaret pierces the sky

PRIZREN, KOSOVO

SHOESTRING Kosovo's second city, Prizren is an attractive place dating back to the Bronze Age. The successive regimes – Roman, Byzantine, Ottoman, Yugoslav, Kosovan – have all their mark on the city, from hilltop fortresses to churches and mosques, all scattered around the Prizren River. Begin with an exploration of the castle, fortified since at least the Roman period, though much of what remains today is from the Ottoman era. Walk the battlements for fantastic city views, then descend into town to visit the beautifully decorated Sinan Pasha Mosque. Cross the gorgeous sixteenth--century stone-arched bridge, and head for the Serbian Orthodox Church of Our Lady of Ljeviš, adorned with magnificent medieval frescoes.

Stay: Prizren is peppered with welcoming and centrally located hostels, such as *Ura* and *Bushati*, as well as a clutch of affordable hotels.

Eat: A great selection of budget restaurants are strung along the river's south bank beneath the fortress, serving everything from Italian to Kosovan food.

Drink: Once the sun goes down, head to *Te Kinezi*, a small, friendly bar where you can knock back local *rakia* (brandy) and craft beers until the small hours.

The Church of Holy Saviour clings to the hillside

Traditional Kosovan pie

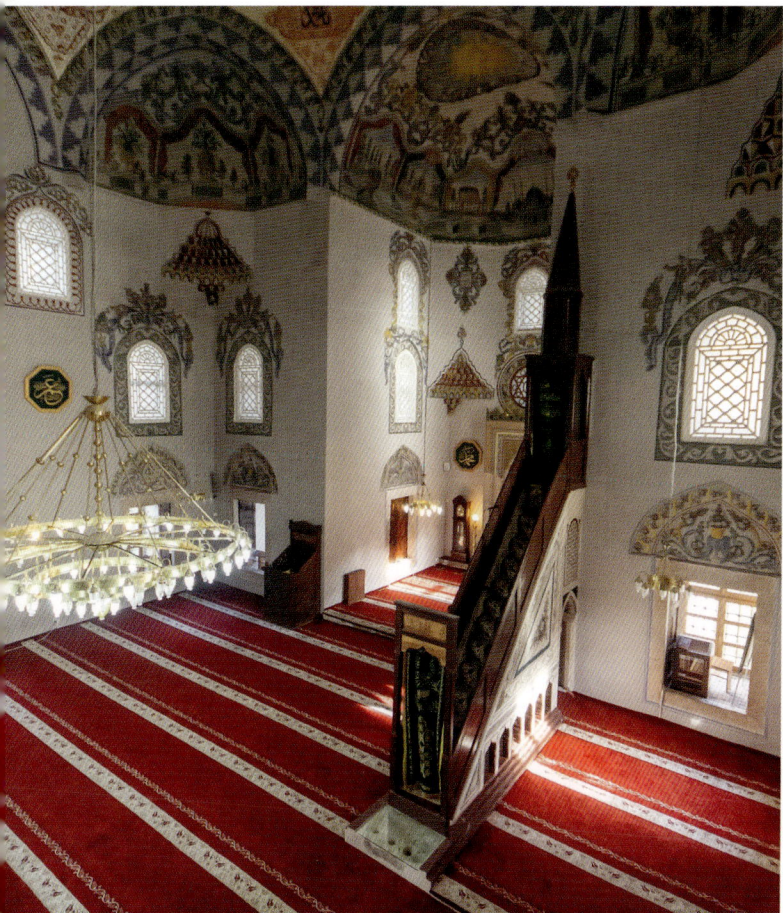
Ottoman-era Sinan Pasha Mosque

The hilltop Prizren Fortress dates to the Bronze Age

Lake Pehoé, Torres del Paine National Park

Humpback whale in the Strait of Magellan

Perito Moreno Glacier in Argentina

Local liquor made from the calafate berry

PATAGONIA, CHILE/ARGENTINA

SAVE Once seen, never forgotten: Patagonia's end-of-the-world landscapes are truly epic. Granite spires poke above primeval forest, turning blood-red in the first light of dawn. Humpback and blue whales breach among the icebergs of mist-shrouded fjords. Vast glaciers spew off the Patagonian Ice Sheet, to calve (all too frequently, due to global warming) into turquoise lakes. Nowhere epitomises the stunning wilds of Patagonia more than the iconic Torres del Paine National Park in Chile and Los Glaciares National Park in Argentina. The 140km Torres del Paine Circuit is one of the finest treks on the planet; the shorter 'W' route takes in the highlights. The Mt Fitzroy area of Los Glaciares is closer to a true wilderness experience, with only camping for intrepid hikers.

Stay: Be sure to prebook campsites, *refugios* and lodges in Torres del Paine.

Eat: *Refugios* will usually serve hot meals to guests at an additional charge.

Drink: Try a cocktail containing the calafate berry, which has cultural significance for the region's Indigenous peoples who believe — *El que come calafate ha de volver* (Those who taste it are guaranteed to return).

Musée d'Orsay, a cultural heavyweight

Fondation Louis Vuitton, the brainchild of Frank Gehry

Montmartre is dotted with pavement bistros

Le Bristol is the city's hottest address

PARIS, FRANCE

SPLURGE Paris, in the movies and on the TV screen, can be a world of clichés. But there's no denying the city has a magical quality. It's an outstanding cultural centre, with its impressive buildings – not least Frank Gehry's stunning Fondation Louis Vuitton – and unparalleled art, nightlife and ethnic diversity. Montmartre is home to some of the best jazz bars on the planet – all serving the finest rouge and slabs of cheese, naturally. With a plethora of standout museums – think Musée d'Orsay, Centre Pompidou, the underrated Dalí Paris and of course the Louvre – Paris has an unrivalled cultural legacy.

Stay: Among the city's most iconic hotels, Le Bristol opened in 1925; another landmark institution is Le Meurice (Picasso married here, Salvador Dalí lived here).
Eat: The delicate, Michelin-starred Chinese-French fusion food at elegantly simple yam'Tcha is outstanding.
Drink: The luxury Four Seasons Hotel George V's bar, with velvet Louis XVI style chairs, wood panelling and a glittering chandelier, is a sumptuous place for heady cocktails.

Centre Pompidou

Q

The Petit Champlain district is littered with bistros

QUÉBEC CITY, CANADA

SHOESTRING With its Unesco-protected old town, diverse museums and local cuisine, the fortified Québec City is the perfect place to experience French-Canadian culture. Historic sites like the Morrin Centre library and the elegant nineteenth-century Parliament Building are worth a visit, and many museums waive entry fees on the first Sunday of each month. The best way to see Vieux Québec is on foot, strolling from the city walls to narrow, cobbled streets like rue du Cul-de-Sac. Join a free walking tour to learn more – but don't forget to tip. Québec City is on the traditional and unceded lands of the Huron-Wendat people, and no visit is complete without delving into the Nation's culture; start with the Huron-Wendat Museum and immersive Onhwa'Lumina night walk.

Stay: The *Auberge Internationale de Québec* has dorms and private rooms, and its old-town address makes it one of the best-located budget options.

Eat: Poutine is the must-try street food when visiting Québec. *Chez Ashton* is a local institution, while *Poutineville* is popular for its create-your-own menu.

Drink: Try L'Inox microbrewery for craft beers, or cosy *Bar Ste-Angèle* for well-priced drinks and live jazz.

The nineteenth-century Parliament Building

Poutine, Québec's favourite street food

The Morrin Centre library is a national historic site

Huron-Wendat Nation woman in ceremonial dress

Manhattan views from Queens

Queens Pride parade in Jackson Heights

Jackson Heights, a multicultural enclave in Queens

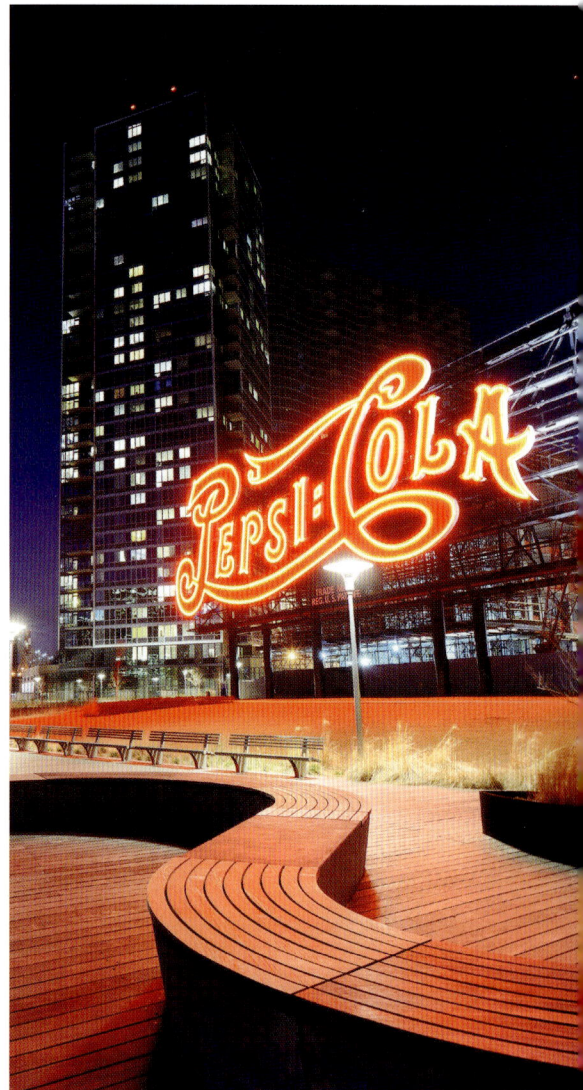

Gantry Plaza State Park

QUEENS, USA

SAVE New York's biggest borough delivers on global food, top-notch museums and fine views of that famous Manhattan skyline – best taken in from the Long Island City Promenade. A walking tour is a great way to get to grips with Queens: guides from Streetwise will take you into the heart of Jackson Heights, where colourful Latin American bakeries sit alongside Indian and Nepalese restaurants. To the east, Flushing lays claim to one of the world's most vibrant Chinatowns, thick with Asian supermarkets, karaoke bars, herbalists and Chinese eateries. The joy is in wandering, but on drizzly days, there are some inviting museums too: the Museum of the Moving Image dives into the art of filmmaking, while MoMA PS1 is a home for avant-garde art installations.

Stay: In Queens' up-and-coming Long Island City neighbourhood, *Boro Hotel* promises sleek, minimalist rooms and a rooftop bar with views of Manhattan.

Eat: Foodies are spoilt for choice in Queens. Top picks include *Tacoway Beach* for stellar fish tacos, and *Stamatis*, one of Astoria's great Greek restaurants.

Drink: On a sunny day, beeline for the patios at *The Jar Bar* or *Bohemian Hall*.

Plaza de San Francisco

Ciudad Vieja unfurling from El Panecillo

Iglesia la Compañía de Jesús illuminated for a festival

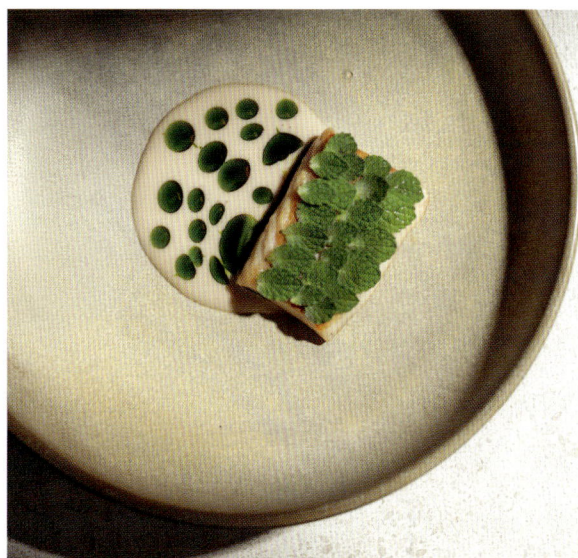
Everyday life unfolds at Plaza de San Francisco

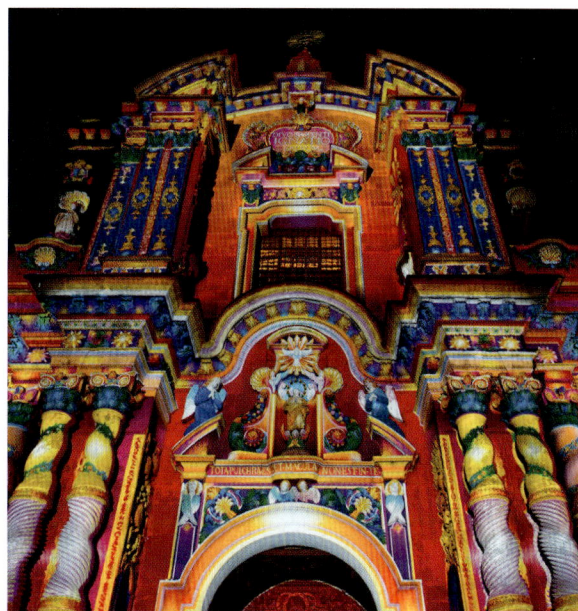
Culinary art at *Nuema*

QUITO, ECUADOR

SPLURGE At 2850m above sea level, Quito – or Carita de Dios (God's Little Face) – is one of the highest cities in South America. A rich cultural mishmash whose beginnings were founded by the Inca, the Ecuadorian capital has an abundance of well-kempt colonial architecture, best seen in its Unesco-listed Ciudad Vieja (Old Town). Delve into the abundance of churches for an art escape; the Iglesia la Compañía de Jesús houses a fantastic collection of Baroque works. And don't miss the city's botanical garden and arboretum.

Stay: Rest your head at boutique hotel *Casa Gangotena*.

Eat: Try the tasting menu by Alejo Chamorro and Pía Salazar at award-winning *Nuema* for a flavour of Ecuador's diverse ingredients from the Pacific to the Amazon.

Drink: Savour a digestif at *Ñukanchikwan Taki*, a rooftop bar at cool *Hotel Otavalo* with fabulous city views.

R

Palace of the Grand Master of the Knights

The catch of the day ends up on restaurant menus

Clouds of bougainvillea in Lindos

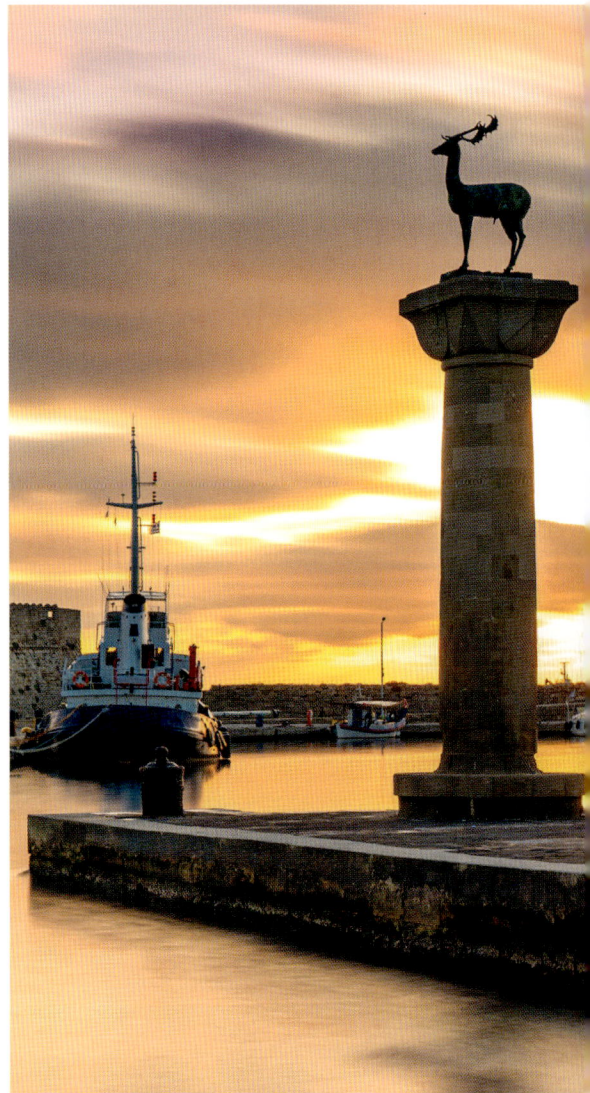

Mandraki Harbour

RHODES, GREECE

SHOESTRING Rhodes is packed with cultural sites, from its Unesco-awarded historic core to the clifftop acropolis at Lindos and the unique Butterfly Valley – where a rare species gravitates in early summer. Throw in 300 days of sunshine a year and a beach-bejewelled coastline, and it's easy to see why the largest Dodecanese island is a popular holiday destination. It costs nothing to wander the cobbled alleyways of the Old Town. Be sure to visit the Palace of the Grand Master of the Knights of Rhodes; buy a combined ticket for the Archaeological Museum and entry to the palace is free.

Stay: Try *Olympos Pension*, with its lovely courtyard and well-priced doubles and triples, or *Stay Hostel* for dorm and private rooms and a basement cinema.

Eat: Vegetarians and vegans will love meat-free *ONO by Marouli*, while carnivores should head to *Niohori* for roast lamb or village sausage.

Drink: Chill out after a day's sightseeing in *The Walk Inn* where locals and visitors rub shoulders over a pint of beer or glass of wine.

RYE, ENGLAND

SAVE Clinging to a hill above Romney Marsh, Rye is a charming huddle of half-timbered, wonky buildings. Independents reign supreme here, with its cluster of boutique shops; try *The Confit Pot* and *Puckhaber* for antiques, *McCully & Crane* for art, and *Rye Old Books* for tomes. Check out Lamb House, home to author Henry James and, later, EF Benson, and climb St Mary's Church for fine views. Visit in February for Rye Bay Scallop Week or September for the two-week Arts Festival.

Stay: Book a room at *The George*, a former coaching inn with a wood-beamed bar.

Eat: After a long stroll along Camber Sands, stop for slow-cooked beef brisket or a bowl of delicious smoked fish chowder from *Tatner's* food truck.

Drink: *Knoops* only offers one thing – hot chocolate – but it does it with style. Choose your chocolate (from 27 to 80 percent solids), add your extras (spices, peppers, fruits, even flowers, or a shot of something stronger) and enjoy.

Mermaid Street, Rye's most photographed lane

The River Tillingham flows around Rye

McCully & Crane art gallery and shop

Knoops, the place to go for hot chocolate

St Peter's Basilica rising above St Angelo Bridge

Michelin-starred dishes at *Glass Hostaria*

Galleria Doria Pamphilj

Five-star luxury at *Hotel de Russie*

ROME, ITALY

SPLURGE There's just something about Rome: its grandeur, its long-living history, its world-renowned cultural legacy. Beyond the big tourist draws a treasure trove awaits curious travellers: duck into the extraordinary Galleria Doria Pamphilj to take in works by Caravaggio, Breughel, Titian, Raphael and Velásquez, before browsing the chic boutiques lining nearby Via dei Condotti. Step into the art-rich churches of Santa Maria del Popolo, Sant'Agostino and San Luigi dei Francesi to find more splendid Caravaggios. See a different side to the city by signing up for a Scooteroma tour to zip around the Colosseum and sights outside the Centro Storico by Vespa or book a private guided tour with a historian (www.understandingrome.com) to make even a visit to the notoriously crowded Vatican Museums and St Peter's Basilica a breeze.

Stay: Coolly elegant *Hotel de Russie* is the abode of choice for the jet set, while *Palazzo Dama* is gloriously whimsical with an air of glamour; the outdoor pool and bar is a chic hangout.

Eat: Trastevere's smartest dining option is Michelin-starred *Glass Hostaria*, helmed by Italian uber-chef Cristina Bowerman.

Drink: Campo de' Fiori, Monti, Trastevere and Testaccio are the densest and most happening parts of town for a night out; simply follow the locals to the action.

Vespa tours take in ancient sites beyond the Centro Storico

S

SAMARKAND, UZBEKISTAN

SHOESTRING Few names are as evocative as Samarkand, with its associations of a rich Eastern kingdom and key stopover on the Silk Road. The reality lives up to the expectation: the city's historic streets are packed with gorgeous mosques and tombs. The jewel in the crown is the Registan, a beautiful open space flanked by three blue-domed madrassahs. To the north is the hulking Bibi-Khanym Mosque, commissioned by Timur and intended to be epic. The construction of this magnificent building proved too ambitious, however, and it soon fell into ruin, though its tiled facades – restored by the Soviets – remain glorious. Timur himself is buried in the Gur-e-Amir Mausoleum, and further richly decorated tombs can be seen in the necropolis of Shah-i-Zinda.

Stay: *Jahongir Hotel* has meticulously furnished rooms set around a courtyard, while *Hotel Minor* is crowned by a rooftop terrace with Registan views.

Eat: Uzbekistan's signature dish is *plov*, a cumin-spiked mix of rice, meat and vegetables: ask for it at *Labi G'or*.

Drink: Stop by one of Samarkand's many *chaikhanas* (teahouses) for a pot of Central Asian green tea, served in an iconic Uzbek blue-and-white tea set.

Ornate tiled facade of Ulugh Beg Madrassah

Uzbek traditional dish *plov*

Gur-e-Amir, the mausoleum of Turco-Mongol conqueror Timur

Bride and groom in traditional Uzbek costume at Registan

The minaret-studded skyline of Sarajevo

Sarajevo Tunnel, used for obtaining supplies during the Bosnian War

Sarajevo Cable Car whisks passengers up Trebević

Baščaršija is the place to go for traditional Bosnian coffee

Pavement cafés flank the streets

SARAJEVO, BOSNIA AND HERZEGOVINA

SAVE Intriguing culture, fine architecture, tempting cuisine: Sarajevo has it all. Wander around Baščaršija, the city's fifteenth-century core where copper-smiths chip away at intricate designs, and vendors display colourful kilim rugs. Gain an understanding of the tragic siege of Sarajevo at the Tunnel Museum, where you can duck into the 800m-long tunnel that locals dug by hand in 1992 to obtain food, aid and supplies during the Bosnian War. For fine views, hop on the cable car at the foot of Mount Trebević – host to the 1984 Winter Olympics.

Stay: The Aziza and President hotels are good budget digs.

Eat: Hotfoot it to Željo if you want to try çevapi (grilled meat) – the national dish is the only item on the menu.

Drink: Brkić Winery in Čitluk was opened by Josip Brkić's family in 1979, though it wasn't until after the fall of Yugoslavia in 1994 that wineries could sell to the public.

The hilltop Hohensalzburg Fortress

SALZBURG, AUSTRIA

SPLURGE A cake-like confection of Baroque domes, fountain-splashed piazzas and colonnaded courtyards, Salzburg could almost be a piece of Italy plonked in the Alps. The birthplace of Mozart, Salzburg offers a wealth of sights linked to the music icon, as well as the irresistible Mozartkugeln chocolates that carry his name. The city's fine churches and palaces encapsulate the artistic glories of the Austrian past. Stroll the warren-like streets of the Old Town to glimpse this architectural legacy and swing by the ornamental gardens at the Mirabell and Hellbrunn palaces.

Stay: Overlooking the historic St Sebastian's Cemetery, *Altstadthotel Wolf Dietrich* excels in plush rooms and attention-to-detail service.

Eat: Hidden within St Peter's Abbey, deep in the Old Town, *St Peter Stiftskulinarium* pairs contemporary cuisine with fine wine in a history-steeped location.

Drink: Augustiner-Bräu has brewed beer in this Augustinian monastery since 1621, and Salzburg's most noble beverage is served here today in archaic mugs.

irabell Palace gardens

ugustiner-Bräu brewery is set in a former monastery

Mozartkugeln chocolates

T

TBILISI, GEORGIA

SHOESTRING The 20m-high sculpture of Mother Georgia watches benevolently over Tbilisi, bearing a cup of wine in one hand, a drawn sword in the other – a nod to the country's warm hospitality as well as its stoutness in the face of invaders. The city unfurls before the proud statue, tumbling down the hillside to the Old Town, a tangle of evocative eighteenth-century lanes. Here, Anchiskhati Basilica, the city's oldest church, is painted with time-faded medieval frescoes. To the west, the Soviet-built Rustaveli Avenue is home to the excellent Georgian National Museum. Throughout Tbilisi, a playful street art scene features everything from giant bicycle sculptures to street light maintenance workers.

Stay: *Envoy Hostel* has dorms and private rooms, plus a roof terrace with city views; the team are more than happy to arrange tours for guests.

Eat: A highlight of any trip to Georgia is the food: the country is justly proud of its culinary traditions. Try *khachapuri*, bread baked with cheese, herbs and egg, but save room for dessert at one of Tbilisi's many ice-cream parlours.

Drink: Georgia is famed for its excellent, affordable wines. One of the most atmospheric and friendly bars to sample a glass or two is *Karalashvili Wine Cellar*.

Old Tbilisi is an enchanting huddle of painted houses

Tbilisi's Old Town

Georgia is famed for its fine wines

Mother Georgia gazes out over the city

The rose-tinted streets of Toulouse

Cité de l'espace

Capitole de Toulouse

Grilled Toulouse sausage is a local speciality

Street musician in the Pink City

TOULOUSE, FRANCE

SAVE La Ville Rose, or the Pink City, is strung along the banks of the Garonne in southwest France. Café-lined place du Capitole is a popular meeting point and a great spot to see Toulouse's famous pink-red bricks glow at sunset. Visit on Wednesday for the bustling market, or at Christmas for food stalls serving warming bowls of *aligot*, silk-smooth cheesy mashed potatoes. Elsewhere, Musée Saint-Raymond is packed with archaeological finds, while Cité de l'espace brings alive the fascinating field of spaceflight.

Stay: Right by the market and steps from the Capitole, *Ours Blanc* is one of the city's better bargains.

Eat: Take your pick from the row of mezzanine restaurants above the food market in place Victor-Hugo.

Drink: *Au Père Louis* opened its doors in 1889 and has hardly changed since; try the signature *quinquina* aperitif.

Neon lights in Kabukicho

TOKYO, JAPAN

SPLURGE Tokyo is an intriguing blend of old and new. One moment, you might be wandering past the temples, craft shops and traditional inns of Asakusa; the next, you'll be left reeling by the frenetic, neon-soaked streets of Harajuku; the same day, you could hike the iconic Mount Fuji surrounded by nothing other than tumbling natural landscapes. To immerse yourself in Japanese culture, set aside time to explore the vast National Art Center; enjoy *kabuki*, *nō* and *bunraku* puppetry at the National Theatre; and wander the Rikugien, a beautiful garden designed to reflect scenes from ancient Japanese poetry. Visit in late March/early April to join the hanami parties beneath the cherry blossom trees in Ueno Park, around the Imperial Palace moat or along the Meguro-gawa.

Stay: Bed down in *Hoshinoya* for a luxe spin on a traditional *ryokan*; highlights include an intimate ten-table restaurant and the seventeenth-floor *onsen*.

Eat: You'll need to book weeks in advance to nab a table at *Hakkoku* for a taste of uber-chef Hiroyuki Sato's thirty-piece omakase sushi menu.

Drink: City big-hitters include *Benfiddich*, *The SG Club* and *Memento Mori*.

Tokyo skyline against the backdrop of Mount Fuji

Life-size doll at Edo-Tokyo Museum

Sensō-ji, a Buddhist temple in Asakusa

Rikugien garden reflects scenes from Japanese poetry

U

ULLAPOOL, SCOTLAND

SHOESTRING The largest town in Northwest Scotland, Ullapool's salty authenticity owes much to its fabulous position across a sheltered arm of land in Loch Broom and its long-standing reputation as a key fishing centre; after all, it was founded by the British Fisheries Society at the height of the herring boom in 1788. Community life, including fishing and crofting, is sensitively recalled in the Ullapool Museum. Strike out to the Summer Isles, a cluster of uninhabited islets a couple of miles offshore, to sight seabird colonies, dolphins and porpoises, or venture further afield to the Isle of Lewis, with its promise of true wilderness.

Stay: Get a comfy night's kip at *Ullapool Youth Hostel* or pitch up (literally) at *Ardmair Point*, a tidy campsite dramatically positioned on the peninsula north of town. *Caledonian Hotel* on the waterfront is a good bet if you have deeper pockets.

Eat: For a taste of some of Scotland's finest seafood, head to the *Seafood Shack*; the menu depends on that day's catch (think scallops, lobster burger, crab claws).

Drink: The ever-popular *Ferry Boat Inn* offers a decent pint, but *Ceilidh Place* is the place to go for live music.

Ullapool has a strong fishing heritage

Caledonian Hotel overlooks Loch Broom

Resident seals bask on Ullapool's rocky coastline

Old painted fishing boats bob in the water

The majestic City Palace

UDAIPUR, INDIA

SAVE Udaipur is a fairytale city sheltered among the forest-swathed hills of the Aravalli Range in Rajasthan. Centrepiece of the city is the beautiful Lake Pichola, ringed by whitewashed palaces and *havelis* (townhouses), with the dreamy *Taj Lake Palace* appearing to float magically in the middle of the water. Boat trips are an essential part of any itinerary, as are visits to the City Palace, whose towering walls conceal some of Rajasthan's most exquisite interiors – a glimpse into the regal lifestyles of former *maharajas* (princes). Myriad further attractions include the historic Jagdish Temple and the absorbing Bagore-ki-Haveli Museum, home to the world's largest turban.

Stay: Book a lake-facing heritage room at *Jagat Niwas*, a charming hotel spread across a pair of historic *havelis* in the heart of the city and brimming with Rajasthani character.

Eat: Close to all the main attractions, *Jaiwana Haveli* is an unpretentious rooftop restaurant offering superb lake views alongside a good selection of affordably priced Indian fare.

Drink: Linger over a sundowner at *Picholi Bar*, enjoying a peerless location on historic Jag Mandir island in the middle of Lake Pichola.

Musician on the banks of Lake Pichola

Rajasthani thali, a feast fit for a prince

Teal-washed interiors of City Palace

Jagdish Temple

The 16m-high Delicate Arch is a natural wonder

Bryce Canyon National Park

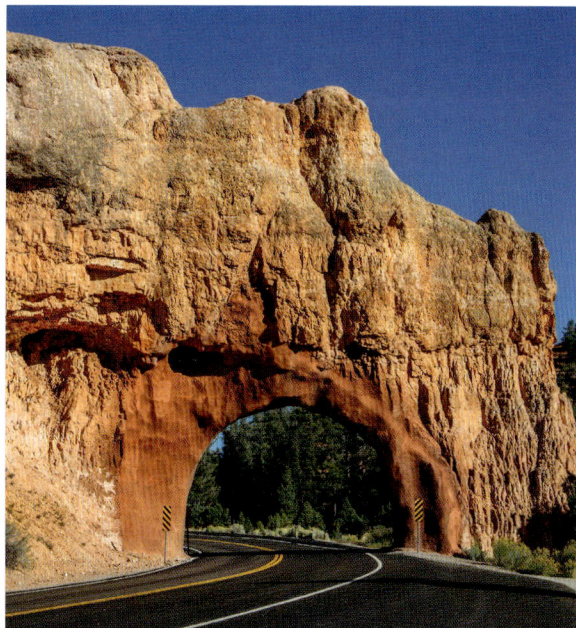
Scenic Byway 12 passes through Red Rock Canyon

alt Lake City

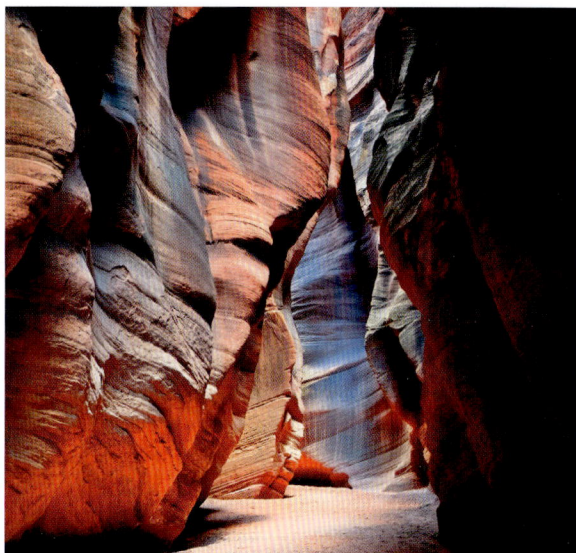
Buckskin Gulch, one of the world's longest slot canyons

UTAH, USA

SPLURGE Driving along Utah's most famous All-American Road — the 123-mile-long Scenic Byway 12 — looming *hoodoos* become ghostly totems, red rock mesas turn into Martian landscapes, and arched canyons conjure ideas of other worlds. Throw in thrilling experiences such as e-biking Bryce Canyon National Park, canyoning in Escalante and llama-trekking at Capitol Reef National Park, nd you'll quickly see why an adventure in Utah is unparalleled. It's the Southwest at its most colourful too — expect vibrant gorges, golden arches and sunburnt-orange slot canyons — and it promises the storied desert towns, swanky restaurants and extravagant roadside accommodations to match.

Stay: A few minutes' drive outside Escalante is *Yonder*, a footloose desert resort with glamping cabins, retro drive-in cinema and luxury Airstream trailers.

Eat: *Hunt & Gather* in the cactus-fringed town of Torrey near Capitol Reef offers slow-cooked wild game and fish.

Drink: *Stone Hearth Grille* pairs T-bones and Napa Valley reds with epic views of the Grand Staircase-Escalante.

V

Basilica of St Stanislaus

Basilian Gate, Monastery of the Holy Trinity

The tiny, self-proclaimed Republic of Užupis in Vilnius

Traditional Lithuanian potato pancakes

VILNIUS, LITHUANIA

SHOESTRING Nestling in a bowl of low hills, Vilnius is one of the most attractive cities in Northern Europe, its winding alleys lined with pastel-hued houses; Baroque belfries looming over every corner. Stroll the Lithuanian capital's streets to stumble across craft shops, cute cafés and quirky museums. Set-piece sights include the Neoclassical cathedral and its lighthouse-like belfry, and the nearby Ducal Palace, which recalls the days when the Grand Duchy of Lithuania was a major European power, stretching from the Baltic to the Black Sea. There's a burgeoning culture of tasty, inexpensive street food, with traditional potato pancakes joined by a growing crop of veggie bites and fusion recipes.

Stay: The *Mai Ram Yoga House* offers cute en suites in tranquil setting – downward dogs optional.

Eat: Globe-spanning inspiration goes into the plant-based brunches and lunches at *RoseHip Vegan Bistro*, best washed down with an energising fruit cocktail.

Drink: It's often a squeeze to get into cramped bar *Wh Hit John*, but this lively hangout offers the perfect introduction to the city's bohemian underbelly.

The Three Crosses Monument is a symbol of national identity

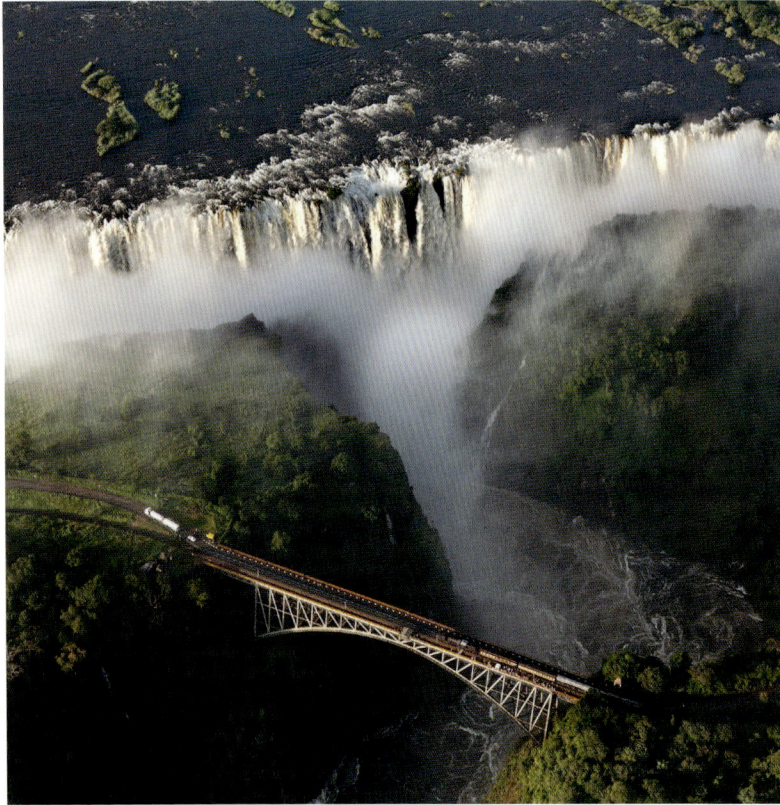

Helicopters offer a luxury (and dry) tour

Bungee jumping from the bridge

Sunlit spray and rainbows

Mettle-testing adrenaline sports

VICTORIA FALLS, ZIMBABWE

SAVE The energy and power of over a mile's width of the Zambezi River thundering 100m down a sheer chasm is a compelling sight and, combined with the clouds of sunlit spray and rainbows, reason enough to spend a day or two gazing at Victoria Falls. For closer views, you can take a river cruise, or simply walk or cycle up the river towards the Zambezi National Park. The world's most adrenaline-charged whitewater rafting and riverboarding trips surge through the gorge beneath the Falls, while bungee jumpers plunge from the bridge overhead. As if that's not enough, there's abseiling, cable-sliding or high-wiring in one of the Batoka gorges.

Stay: *Shoestrings Backpackers*, just 500m from town, is a fun hostel with a lovely pool, while the popular *Victoria Falls Rest Camp* is set in spotless grounds 2km from town and offers basic rooms, six-person cottages and pitches.

Eat: The central *Ilala Lodge* rustles up an excellent Mongolian barbecue.

Drink: Beer halls at the *Town Council Rest Camp* and near the Chinotimba taxi ranks are the places to meet Zimbabweans.

The grand Rococo facade of Schönbrunn Palace

Kunst Haus Wien, designed by Friedensreich Hundertwasser

Kaiserschmarrn (shredded pancakes)

Gilded bronze statue of Johann Strauss II, Stadtpark

Palmenhaus, a foliage-filled restaurant

VIENNA, AUSTRIA

SPLURGE From awe-inspiring architecture to classical music and chocolate torte, Vienna is steeped in decadence. One of the city's most iconic buildings is the vast Rococo Schönbrunn Palace, with over 1400 lavishly decorated rooms and huge gardens sheltering a maze, an orangery, a huge greenhouse and even a zoo. Vienna is also known for its coffeehouse culture; one of the city's finest cafés is the nineteenth-century *Demel*, where you can see chefs whipping up Kaiserschmarrn (fluffy shredded pancakes) through the windows.

Stay: Kip at *Do & Co Vienna*, a boutique hotel overlooking the zigzagging mosaic-tiled roof of St Stephen's Cathedral.

Eat: Grab a bite to eat at *Palmenhaus*, a greenhouse-turned-restaurant filled with lush foliage; in summer, people throng the outside terrace overlooking Burggarten park.

Drink: Sip a Warhol daiquiri in the Art Deco *Kleinod*, to a cool soundtrack of Twenties jazz and early soul music.

W

WHITBY, ENGLAND

SHOESTRING If there's one essential stop on the North Yorkshire coast it's Whitby, with its historical associations, evocative ruins and charming fishing harbour. Watched over by a seventh-century clifftop abbey, the river-threaded town is split into two halves: the cobbled Old Town to the east, and the newer (mostly eighteenth- and nineteenth-century) enclave known as West Cliff. The town has curious literary connections: think blood-sucking vampire. Drawing on his own knowledge of Whitby, Bram Stoker built a story mixing legend and fact: the grounding of Count Dracula's ship on Tate Hill Sands was based on a real news report about the shipwreck of a Russian vessel, the *Dmitry*, beneath East Cliff. Fans can visit the abbey, church and steps, and graveyard from the novel.

Stay: *YHA Whitby* is set in a Grade I-listed building with fine views.

Eat: You'll be hard-pressed to pick from the many options at *Humble Pie* – steak, stout and leek, Romany, Homity, haggis and neep; all served with mash and peas.

Drink: The *Black Horse* is a lovely, part seventeenth-century pub in the old town.

The characterful Whitby Harbour

Whitby Goth Weekend is a biannual event

Whitby is flanked by a pair of lighthouse-topped piers

Clifftop ruins of Whitby Abbey

Palace on the Isle, Royal Baths Park

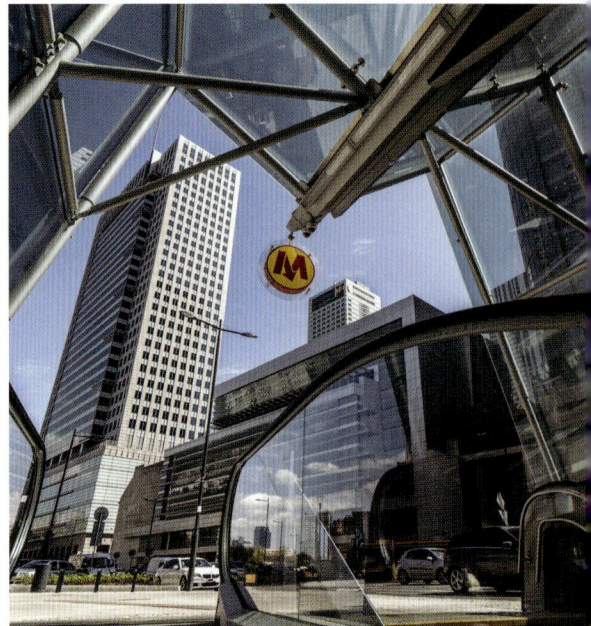
The contemporary face of Warsaw

Vistula's west bank is strung with barge bars

Sigismund Column on Castle Square

WARSAW, POLAND

SAVE Warsaw is an ever-changing metropolis that combines Old Town charm with Stalinist-era Baroque and the gleaming corporate towers of today. Deeply scarred by World War II and profoundly marked by communist rule, the Polish capital was embroiled in the turmoil of the twentieth century, as recalled in the Warsaw Uprising Museum, Katyń Museum and Museum of the History of Polish Jews. There's more to Warsaw than history, though. It is a city of destination restaurants, riverside beaches, bar-filled bohemian quarters, and hands-on attractions like the Copernicus Science Centre. It is also a city of intriguing curiosities: look out for the plastic palm tree on Aleje Jerozolimskie, Warsaw University Library's roof garden, and the incandescent Neon Museum.

Stay: Quirky but comfy B&Bs are a Warsaw speciality, with the likes of *Apple Inn* and *Autor Rooms* providing designer comforts in downtown postcodes.

Eat: Eat lunch inside the book-filled *Café Kafka* or nab a deckchair on the lawn.

Drink: The west bank of the Vistula River is strung with open-air bars, many offering live music and street-food trucks.

Staggering sunsets in this corner of the world

WHITSUNDAYS, AUSTRALIA

SPLURGE A scattering of subtropical islands just off the Queensland coast, the Whitsundays encompasses much that is most spectacular about seaside luxury. Beachcombing, sailing, diving, cocktail-supping and gourmet dining: myriad attractions lure well-heeled visitors to the archipelago's swish hotels and marinas. The Whitsundays is also the main launchpad for the Great Barrier Reef, with boat trips offering a close encounter with the area's rich marine life, whether snorkelling among fanning coral, swimming with turtles or soaking up the scene from a cushion-topped deck. The main settlement of Airlie Beach offers bathing, boating and clubbing galore, although a handful of quieter islands offers a more tranquil take on the lotus-eating experience.

Stay: The self-catering apartments at *Peninsula Airlie Beach* offer chic gallery-white interiors and floor-to-ceiling-windows overlooking the marina.

Eat: It's worth making the trip to Hamilton Island to seek out *Bommie*, famed for its freshly caught seafood and extravagant desserts.

Drink: Alfresco cocktail bar *One Tree Hill* on Hamilton Island offers sweeping views and is a good spot to catch the sunset.

Dive into the underwater playground

Fish D'vine, Airlie Beach

Postcard-perfect scenes

Sailing in the Whitsundays

X

Tal-Mixta Cave, best visited at sunset

XAGĦRA, GOZO

SHOESTRING A short ferry ride from Malta, Gozo is a small island studded with gnarled olive trees and dotted with tiny sandstone villages. Explore its rocky landscape on two wheels, cycling down country roads and pausing whenever a grand church or coastal vista catches your eye. Base yourself in Xagħra, where the pace slips down a few gears. The red-tinged sands of Ramla Beach are a perfect place to while away an afternoon, before hiking to Tal-Mixta Cave to watch the sunset. Inland, swing by Ta'Mena vineyard for olive oil and wine – with free tastings. And, of course, visit the area's biggest attraction: the Neolithic temples of Ġgantija, almost a millennium older than the Great Pyramid of Giza.

Stay: With outdoor pools, a sun terrace and serene views over the Gozitan countryside, *DGolden Valley* is a chic bolthole near Ramla Beach.

Eat: Family-run *Tal-Furnar* cooks much of its tasty, simple Maltese food in its 100-year-old stone oven. Don't miss *Gelati Granola* in Marsalforn Bay for gelato.

Drink: Gozo's low-key nightlife is concentrated in Marsalforn and Xlendi. Alternatively, pick up some local wine, artisan beer (try Lord Chambray) or *bajtra* (prickly pear liqueur) to sip on your terrace.

Xagħra drums to a slower beat

Rabbit is a Maltese speciality

Xagħra Parish Church

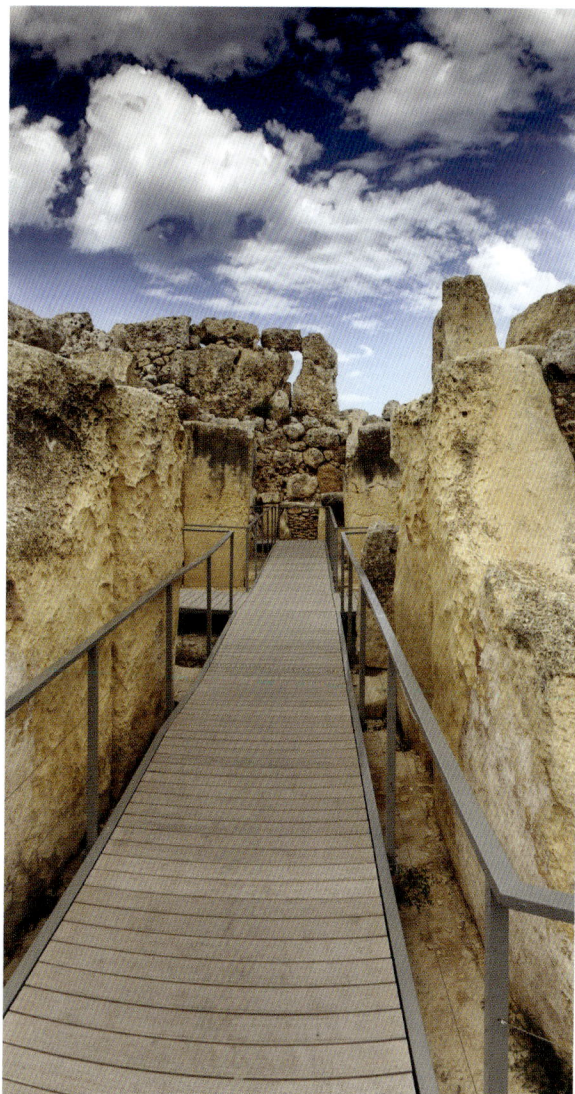

Ġgantija Temples (c. 3600–2500 BC)

Much of Xi'An City Wall has been restored or rebuilt

Xi'an Muslim Quarter

Chinese opera performance

Xi'An City Wall, built in 1370 during the Ming dynasty

XI'AN, CHINA

SAVE One of China's Four Great Ancient Capitals, Xi'An marked the eastern end of the Silk Road — or the beginning of an incredible journey west. The 13.7km-long Xi'An City Wall — the most complete fortifications in China — wraps around the city's ancient core. Enter via one of the four main gates, which mark the cardinal points, to explore the old city on foot, by bike or in a battery car. Set off early the next day to visit one of China's most jaw-dropping sights: the Terracotta Army. Discovered by farmers in 1974, over 8000 clay soldiers, 130 chariots and 670 horses were buried with Qin Shi Huang — the first emperor of China — in 209-210 BCE to protect the ruler in his afterlife.

Stay: Rest your head at *He Designer Hotel*, with futuristic touches such as a red pinpoint stuck into the floor and trees growing from the ceiling.

Eat: Dig into the Muslim market near the Drum Tower to try the meat skewers and flatbreads of the Uyghur, the threatened Islamic community of Xinjiang.

Drink: Affiliated with Xi'an Brewery, *Near Wall Bar* is the only brewpub in the city where you'll find Western-style craft beers.

This quaint city is often overlooked by tourists

The Nestos River wends through Xanthi

The cobblestoned streets of the Old Town

Cathedral of St Sophia The Wisdom of God

XANTHI, GREECE

SPLURGE Often overlooked, Xanthi should be on your radar. This quaint city is built amphitheatrically at the foot of the Rodopi mountains, in the Thrace region of northeastern Greece. The narrow, cobbled streets of the Old Town are lined with Neoclassical mansions and Byzantine churches – an open museum untouched by the years. For more of an insight into the region's heritage, dip into the Folk and History Museum of Xanthi. A fun activity to try is truffle hunting, where you'll go in search of the famed plant. However, the main reason why many Greeks holiday here is the Xanthi Carnival in February, when the streets come alive with parades, floats, musicians and entertainers.

Stay: Bed down at the Belle Epoque-style *1905 Boutique Hotel* – a protected Neoclassical building in the Old Town.

Eat: The gastronomy of the region is eclectic, infused with Balkan and Asia Minor culinary influences. Roasted chickpeas and lamb with local pasta is a popular dish, as are the walnut pies and baklava.

Drink: Wash down dinner with a crisp glass of the local white wine, Roditis.

Xanthi Carnival is a riot of colour and music

The sculpture-peppered Cascade Complex

YEREVAN, ARMENIA

SHOESTRING Armenia's capital is a confident and arty city, with attractive architecture and a lengthy history. Its compact city centre can be explored on foot, beginning with the 2800 fountains and quirky bronze statues in Yerevan's commemorative 2800th Anniversary Park. Wander up to Republic Square, where you'll find magnificent Soviet buildings, and visit the excellent History Museum of Armenia to see, among much else, the world's oldest shoe. Walking north, you'll soon reach the grandiose opera house, beyond which is Yerevan's main calling card, the Cascade Complex: an enormous limestone staircase climbing the hillside, strewn with a collection of remarkable and innovative sculptures. From the plaza at the top, you can admire the view of the entire city, with the great mass of Armenia's sacred mountain, Mt Ararat, looming behind.

Stay: Both *Duck Hostel* and *Kantar* are friendly, welcoming and central.

Eat: Street food such as *lahmacun* (Armenian pizza) and *Zhingyalov hats* (fried flatbreads containing a zingy salad mix) are tasty and inexpensive.

Drink: Don't leave town without visiting the *In Vino* bar: Armenia has been making wine for some 6000 years, and has got very good at it.

Republic Square

Pavement cafés line the streets

Modern art statue

Mt Ararat, a sacred mountain for Armenians

Tunnel View is a scenic viewpoint

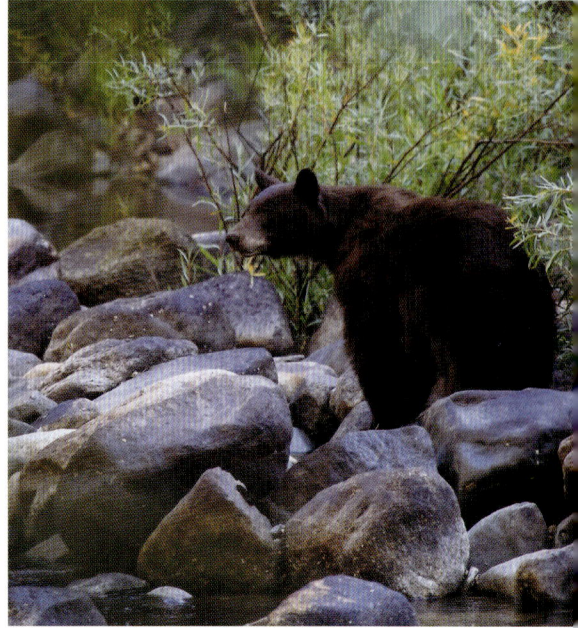

Black bears roam Yosemite National Park

Bring your own kayak if you want to hit the water

Yosemite Falls, one of the world's highest waterfalls

YOSEMITE NATIONAL PARK, USA

SAVE There's not too high a price tag on Yosemite's fine natural bounty. Your $35 vehicle entrance fee is good for seven days, leaving ample time to explore the national park's skyscraping peaks, stooping valleys, waterfalls and canyons. The headline hike is the Half Dome: the trail wriggles out for 25 kilometres, culminating in a scramble up the sheer face of its namesake peak using metal cables. If you've not got a head for heights, there are plenty of viewpoints closer to terra firma: Glacier Point offers unrivalled vistas of Yosemite Valley. Away from the crowded hotspots, the lofty Tuolumne Meadows are laced with quiet hiking trails revealing mineral springs, lakes and epic High Sierra panoramas.

Stay: Nudging an ear-popping 1220m in altitude, *Lower Pines Campground* has creature comforts and is the perfect springboard for hikes in the Yosemite Valley.

Eat: Stock up on supplies before you reach the park and enjoy your provisions at one of the many picnic spots: a favourite is The Cascades area.

Drink: Sink your tipple of choice beneath the stars at your campsite – or beeline for *The Loft at Degnan's* for affordable beer on tap and Californian wines.

YOKOHAMA, JAPAN

SPLURGE Thanks to an open harbour and its low-slung huddle of squat buildings, Japan's second-most populated city feels airier and more spacious than bustling Tokyo. Yokohama's calling card, though, is its Chinatown, founded in 1863 and the largest in the country. The knot of alleyways is lined with 300-plus shops and some 200 restaurants, serving everything from steaming dumplings to succulent dim sum. Foodies should also swing by the fun Cup Noodles Museum, with its interactive displays and gift shop packed with quirky souvenirs.

Stay: Built in the 1920s in European style, the main building of the upmarket *New Grand* retains its original elegance, while rooms in the newer tower offer bay views.

Eat: The famous *Manchinrō* restaurant has been serving tasty Cantonese cuisine since 1892. Though prices are on the high side, the portions are generous.

Drink: *Downbeat* is a dark and edgy jazz club attracting top acts and a fun crowd.

Yokohama's Chinatown is the largest in Japan

sakura-shrouded pagoda in Sankeien Garden

ort of Yokohama

Shin-Yokohama Ramen Museum

Z

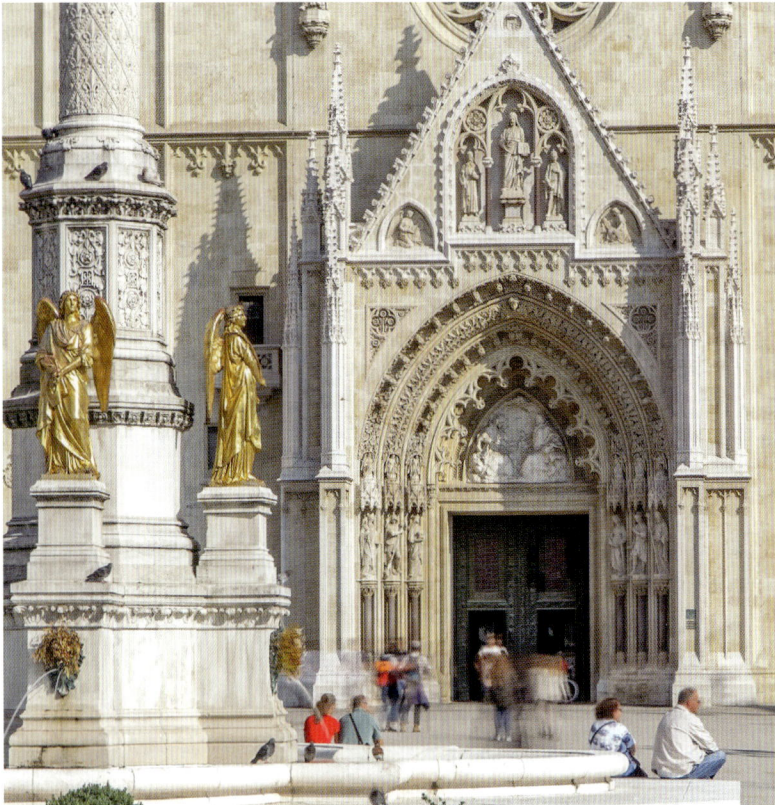

Zagreb Cathedral's Gothic facade

Squid with *blitva* (Swiss chard and potato)

Festival of Lights at Ban Jelačić Square

Zagreb Funicular travels just 66m in distance

ZAGREB, CROATIA

SHOESTRING Croatia's capital is a vibrant city with striking Secessionist architecture, a rich culinary scene and thriving café culture. Zagreb might no longer be Europe's best-kept secret, but it still sees a fraction of the visitors flocking to the Croatian coast and islands. The city's beautiful old core is ripe for exploration: wander the narrow, cobbled streets of Gornji Grad (Upper Town), then take in the elegant facades and green spaces of the Lower Town. Continue on to bustling Dolac Market, Ban Jelačić Square, St Mark's Church with its multicoloured roof tiles, and the neo-Gothic Zagreb Cathedral. Buy a Zagreb Card if you plan to visit several museums – don't miss the Museum of Broken Relationships, Zagreb City Museum and Museum of Contemporary Art.

Stay: Zagreb has accommodation to suit all budgets, including some great hostels; *Swanky Mint* is one of the best, with a top cocktail bar in the garden.

Eat: *Lari i Penati* plates up excellent food in casual surroundings, while traditional *Korčula* turns out delicious fish and seafood; try the squid with *blitva*.

Drink: For excellent local beer, head to craft brewery Pivovara Medvedgrad.

ZAMORA, SPAIN

SAVE Few people have heard of Zamora, let alone know that this walled city has the highest concentration Romanesque architecture in Europe. Dubbed a Unesco World Heritage Site in 2023, the underrated destination has so much to offer in-the-know travellers, and is only an hour from Madrid by high-speed train. Strung along the banks of the Douro River, Zamora is best explored on foot. Must-sees include Zamora Cathedral, with its Byzantine dome, Romanesque tower and Neoclassical cloister; Museo Catedralicio and its time-faded fifteenth-century Flemish tapestries; and the Gothic frescos adorning Capilla de San Ildefonso. Further afield, Lake Sanabria is the largest glacial lake in the Iberian Peninsula, while Toro is a lesser-known wine region behind a delicious full-bodied red.

Stay: Try *Parador de Zamora*, a fifteenth-century palace in the heart of town.

Drink: Don't miss Numanthia, the fine *bodega* that put Toro on the wine map.

Eat: *La Rúa* is the place to go for home cooking; try the *arroz a la zamorana* (rice with pork). *Lera*, an hour from town, is worth the trip for its Michelin-star cuisine.

Unesco-listed Zamora is packed with Romanesque architecture

Stone walls shelter the historic quarter

Holy Week procession

Crooked streets are lined with pastel-hued houses

Stone Town, the capital of Zanzibar

Red-knob starfish are only found in the Indian Ocean

The rare red colobus may be sighted in Jozani Chwaka Bay National Park

Kiwengwa Beach

ZANZIBAR, TANZANIA

SPLURGE Zanzibar, cast adrift in the Indian Ocean 35km off Tanzania's coast, is a favourite post-safari destination. And rightly so: not only does core island Unguja boast blindingly white beaches, but its lesser-trodden siblings – like Pemba and Mafia – have retained an intoxicating off-the-map vibe. But there is so much more to this East African archipelago than being a handy beach add-on for safari-goers. It's a thrilling destination in its own right, from the spice-scented alleys of Unesco-listed Stone Town to excellent diving off the Mnemba Atoll and adventure tours into Jozani Chwaka Bay National Park.

Stay: On Unguja, *Zawadi Hotel* is a collection of twelve villas scattered across a clifftop above Bwejuu Beach, while *Zanzibar White Sand Luxury Villas & Spa*, a sustainably minded Relais & Châteaux property, tumbles down to Paje Beach.

Eat: Feast on a Zanzibari-inspired menu at *Emerson Spice Secret Garden*, though if it's a dramatic location you're after, look no further than *The Rock*, poised on a jagged pinnacle just offshore from Pingwe Beach.

Drink: Pair cocktails with dreamy sunset views at *The 5th at Upendo House*.

INDEX

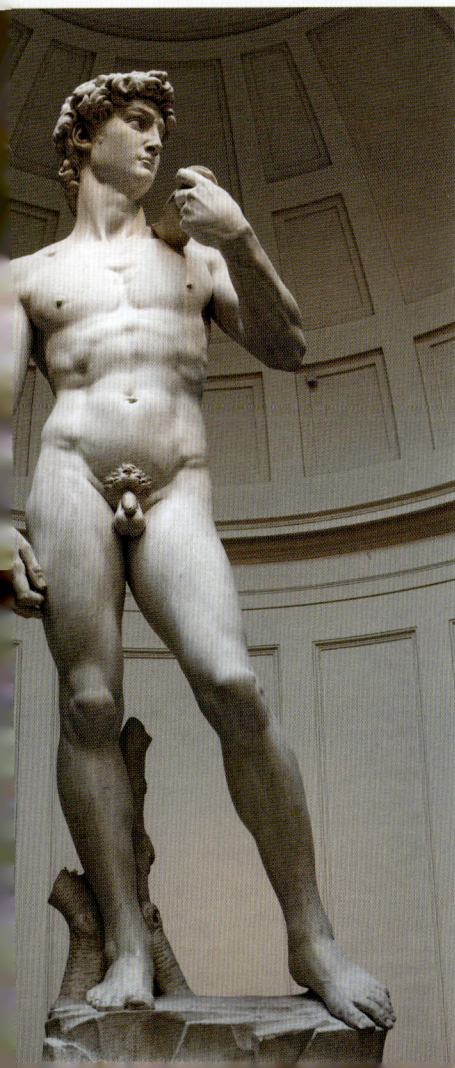

CONTRIBUTORS

Rudolf Abraham

Jacqui Agate

Jonathan Bousfield

Stuart Butler

Kiki Deere

Marco Ferrarese

Rebecca Hall

Rebecca Hallett

Norm Longley

Mike MacEacheran

Lucy McGuire

Sarah Miles

Owen Morton

Sorrel Moseley-Williams

Matthew Pearson

Joanna Reeves

Robert Savage

Zara Sekhavati

Gavin Thomas

Annie Warren

PHOTO CREDITS